BERKLEE PRESS

BELTING

A GUIDE TO
HEALTHY, POWERFUL SINGING

To access audio and video visit:
www.halleonard.com/mylibrary

Enter Code
4718-1747-8522-6718

JEANNIE GAGNÉ

For my wonderful colleagues, my incredibly talented and inspiring students—
who teach me, too—and for my supportive, high-octane, and loving family.

Berklee Press

Editor in Chief: Jonathan Feist
Vice President of Online Learning and Continuing Education/CEO of Berklee Online: Debbie Cavalier
Assistant Vice President of Marketing and Recruitment for Berklee Media: Mike King
Dean of Continuing Education: Carin Nuernberg
Editorial Assistants: Reilly Garrett, Emily Jones, Eloise Kelsey, Zoë Lustri
Technical Vocal Consultant: Douglas F. Roth, M.M., M.A., CCC-SLP
Illustrations for Figures 4.3, II.3.1, and II.10.1: Jeannie Gagné
Author Photo: Mark Stallings
Audio and Video Support: Dylan Wolff
Video Production Advisor: Stephen Gagné

ISBN 978-0-87639-158-7

1140 Boylston Street
Boston, MA 02215-3693 USA
(617) 747-2146
Visit Berklee Press Online at
www.berkleepress.com

Study with

■ BERKLEE ONLINE

online.berklee.edu

DISTRIBUTED BY

HAL•LEONARD®
CORPORATION
7777 W. BLUEMOUND RD. P.O. BOX 13819
MILWAUKEE, WISCONSIN 53213

Visit Hal Leonard Online at
www.halleonard.com

Berklee Press, a publishing activity of Berklee College of Music, is a not-for-profit educational publisher.
Available proceeds from the sales of our products are contributed to the scholarship funds of the college.

CONTENTS

ACKNOWLEDGMENTS

This book would not be possible without the input and talent of many individuals. Thank you to my superb editor Jonathan Feist, whose subtle yet steadfast and on-point suggestions, and patience, are to be commended. Thank you to Molly Low for providing stalwart enthusiasm and a keen eye. Thank you to Mark LaDuke, Jenna Glatt, David Keck, and Erica Leonard for bringing your formidable talent to the videos and being willing to reveal your process. Thank you to Berklee Voice Department Chair Anne Peckham and Assistant Chair Diane Richardson for strongly supporting this book project, and to Douglas Roth MM, MA, CCC-SLP of Tufts Medical Center in Boston for vocal and medical expertise and engaging stories. Thank you to Stephen Gagné and Dylan Wolff for your excellent AV help. And of course, thank you always to my amazing family, for believing in me with gusto while tolerating how many hours I spent tucked away researching, filming, and writing this book.

INTRODUCTION

Singing with a powerful, belted voice is exciting, challenging, and commanding. This way of singing is heard widely throughout popular music, increasingly in the past several years. When practiced wisely, belting can be done healthfully, particularly when it is used as part of an assortment of vocal techniques blended together during a performance. If you are interested in learning how to belt effectively and musically—and without hurting your voice—this book is for you.

Although many singers wish to learn how to belt, there is little written about it. This is probably because belting is difficult to teach well. Many singers and teachers alike misunderstand the physical dynamics involved in healthy belting. They either over-strain their voices or believe incorrectly that one simply cannot belt without harming the voice. As a professional singer, I often belt in my own performances, and have included it in my teaching studio curriculum for over thirty years. After years of continuing study, practice, and research, I have refined an approach for teaching this strong singing style that is consistently successful, offered here to you in *Belting: A Guide to Healthy, Powerful Singing*. Because belting is demanding vocally, this book includes important access to an extensive online library of video and audio examples that illustrate healthy belting, pitfalls to avoid, and useful exercises for you to practice.

Some singers find that their voices take to belting fairly easily, but for others, it is more difficult. If you have been teaching yourself (as I did) how to sing with this robust popular sound, you may find that your efforts are exciting but difficult, perhaps even frustrating. Or, if you belt easily, you may still find that other aspects of your singing are more challenging. Because belting requires strong pressure applied to your (delicate) vocal folds, many voice teachers will not teach it. Though belting is as common in today's popular music as a drummer's backbeat on 2 and 4, many teachers say that it is *always* bad for your voice and should be avoided. This is simply not true. As with anything, there are healthy and not-so-healthy ways to sing. Yes, some singers should belt sparingly, because some voices are less physically resilient than others. (Some people can train to bench-press heavy weights, for example, whereas others have physiques that cannot build that kind of muscle.)

Remember, your voice is unique, arising from a complex blend of your vocal anatomy, thought, movements, and breathing. Just as your face is unique, your singing voice sounds distinctly like *you*. This book will guide you to discover how to belt safely, how to discover what your strengths and limits are, and when you should probably take it easy.

If belting is a goal of yours as a singer, read on! These pages bring you the most up-to-date information about what happens in your voice when you belt, and how to learn to belt in a healthy, sustainable way.

MY STORY

As a naturally high soprano, learning how to belt popular melodies in an alto range did not come easily to me at first. I listened to recordings of singers I admired greatly and attempted to imitate them (the long list includes Chaka Khan, Barbra Streisand, Michael Jackson, Stevie Wonder, Ella Fitzgerald, Sarah Vaughan, Robert Plant, and Laura Nyro). With a higher-toned voice and classical vocal training, I had to teach myself how to sing "big" popular styles effectively and safely. I learned to temper belting with the classical exercises I'd studied in order to maintain my healthy, "neutral" voice (see chapter 1). As a professor of voice at Berklee College of Music, I became very interested in vocal medicine, the physiology of the human voice, and the mental processes that accompany singing. I sought out medical experts in the field, such as voice therapist and professional singer Douglas F. Roth, MM, MA, CCC-SLP of Tufts Medical Center in Boston, Massachusetts. Becoming passionate about performance health, I co-founded and co-directed the Performance Wellness Institute at Berklee, where insightful and gifted faculty continue to offer healthy approaches for playing and singing.

My first book, *Your Singing Voice: Contemporary Techniques, Expression, and Spirit* (Berklee Press, 2012), offers an extensive exploration of using your voice in performance and for pleasure, and describes thoroughly the factual physiology of what happens when you sing. *Belting* picks up where that book left off. It teaches you in living color what students ask me about daily: how can you sing loud, powerful vocals that won't hurt, crack, sound bad, or stop working?

> *"How can you sing loud, powerful vocals that won't hurt, crack, sound bad, or stop working?"*

LEARNING HOW TO BELT EFFECTIVELY

When done well, belting is a dynamic vocal quality that flows effortlessly into an overall flexible and vibrant instrument. When studying any singing style, it is important to honor both the advantages and limitations of your voice's physical structures. The techniques I offer you here are designed to help you learn to identify those structures. They help you discover your unique sound that is reliable and pleasing.

It is imperative that you learn how to belt effectively and sustainably to avoid possible injury, and to recognize the warning signs your body will show you if you are pushing your voice too hard. Belting is not for everyone, nor is belting necessary for all popular singing styles. Nonetheless, do not be afraid of exploring your voice, with all of its colors and options. In spite of what you may have learned to the contrary, there is simply not only one "correct" way to sing.

I wrote this book because there is a tremendous need for it. You have the right to explore your voice in the way that expresses your inner music, your song. In this book, I will not say to you, "That way of singing is wrong, this approach is right." Instead, I offer you guidelines for healthy singing that are supported by proven facts about how the human voice functions.

The approaches presented here work. However, no two people learn in precisely the same way, nor can any physical activity be learned just by reading about it.

Please be sure you watch the videotaped examples provided in the accompanying online videos. They will facilitate your learning immensely.

I recommend filming yourself as you practice. This is an extremely effective learning tool that shows you how your physical experience in the moment compares with the actual filmed results.

You must also practice frequently, through trial-and-error, to reach the result that works. Repetition of anything new is necessary for it to stick, and become habitual.

Finally, you must learn how to know when it's time to rest your voice.

Let's get started.

ABOUT THE ONLINE VIDEO AND AUDIO

To access the accompanying video and audio files, go to www.halleonard.com/mylibrary and enter the code found on the first page of this book. This will grant you instant access to them. Examples with accompanying video or audio are marked with an icon.

PART I

CHAPTER 1

All About Belting

What Is Belting, Exactly?

Simply stated, belting is a type of singing that is robust, bright, and loud. Pitch rises, volume increases. A strong sensation of air pressure comes up from your lungs and through your vocal mechanism, creating the feeling of *pressing* the voice through notes that are becoming more taut as they rise. Then, similar to speaking loudly, belting for contemporary styles typically uses a bright timbre that is placed more "forward" in the mouth when compared with a classical singing approach. Contrary to popular belief, belting is not just about pushing up your "chest voice," as we will see.

We hear belting used commonly today throughout pop, rock, country, musical theater, blues, and R&B songs. Belting conveys strong feeling and can be very dramatic, especially for climactic sections in a song such as the chorus or during other peak moments. The plethora of singing contests on television, including *American Idol* and *The Voice*, reinforce this way of singing by offering a grand prize to the performer who showcases passionate, dramatic, and high-octane singing week after week. These programs seem to say, "If you want to succeed as a singer, belt it out."

It makes sense, then, that learning how to belt is in high demand. Singers are eager to emulate favorite popular artists, to sing with the same charisma and excitement as their musical idols. Belting is all over top 40 stations. Many of today's artists include belting when they sing, and this list of artists is long. Beyoncé, P!nk, Katy Perry, Christina Aguilera, Lady Gaga, Miley Cyrus, Jennifer Hudson, Kesha, and Celine Dion are among the scores of women artists who belt. Among the male artists are Bruce Springsteen, Adam Lambert, Josh Groban, Sting, Steven Tyler of Aerosmith, Matt Bellamy of Muse, Pat Monahan of Train, Prince, and Robert Plant of Led Zeppelin, to name but a few.

WHY *HAS* BELTING BECOME SO POPULAR?

Though musical styles come and go, singing in a belted voice has been around for a long time. While it's not for everyone, belting draws forth our emotions and can be quite thrilling to hear. It is also difficult to do well. Belting is impressive. Inspiring. Energizing. When combined with exciting moments that are accentuated with a performance's instrumentation and theatrical lighting, belting can get audiences to their feet, cheering with raw exhilaration for the singer. Belting is like the mid-court, all-net shot in basketball: extraordinary, bold, and requiring several complementary skills. That is intoxicating to witness! For the singer, the feeling of being applauded with such enthusiasm is seductive. It is a very commanding way to sing, and physically intense. It can be emotionally and physically empowering too, as one's body coordinates a powerful, difficult maneuver before a captivated audience. For the audience, being part of a "happening" where you are drawn into the charisma of an artist who moves you significantly is an unforgettable experience that we want to be a part of. We were there!

Big moments like these in popular songs are golden moments. They build fans. You want to sing along with the artist, you want to *feel* what he or she feels. Belting says, "I am here! I am strong! I can survive this! I am a winner!" These types of affirmations are very seductive and they help songs to become very popular.

BUT...CAN THERE BE TOO MUCH OF A GOOD THING? (LIKE HOT PEPPER IN YOUR COOKING)

How could such an exciting way of singing be overused? Another way to ask the question is: When is it best to belt, and when is it better not to belt?

Because belting is produced with a good deal of pressure in the vocal mechanism, you must be very mindful of vocal health and your own stamina when you sing in this way. I like spicy food sometimes. I like to cook with seasoning. Sometimes, blander food is good, too, because some days, you just want to taste the *food* without so much added seasoning. So, rather than putting hot pepper into every dish I make, I use it more sparingly. Wisely. That makes the meal more special.

The key is to find *balance*. Effective singing is not all about being loud and emotive. ALWAYS BELTING WOULD BE LIKE TYPING THIS BOOK IN ALL CAPITALS AND USING ONLY EXCLAMATION POINTS!!! One way to create balance is by adding dynamic contrast.

Dynamics

Use *dynamics* (changes in volume between softer and louder moments) to keep your listener's attention. Soft passages that are juxtaposed with louder ones, peppered throughout a song, provide a *musical* way to sing, rather than pushing the voice continuously, aiming only for loud volume and excitement. You want to *move* your listeners, to draw them into your performance. You need variation to keep your listeners' attention. Create *events* throughout your song to change it up, rather than performing in a static, linear way. Dynamics help to create events in a song. For example, if I say to you, "I love you," SHOULD I YELL IT? Maybe, sometimes, especially for fun, like standing on the edge of a fountain in a public park (this was a scene in a movie somewhere), proclaiming your love to your best friend. That's when yelling it out could work. But should you *always* yell these so-important words? Personally I would find this extremely off-putting. No thank you. No one wants to be screamed at all the time. At that point, we just tune out. Drama gets old after awhile; people need tenderness, too.

One excellent way to be heard, to spread a message, is to be quieter! Imagine, for example, when a parent successfully captures his or her child's attention. When using a quiet, *intense* tone of voice to say something important, the parent is much more likely to be heard by the child than when the parent is always yelling. (Take it from me, I learned this with my own kids. Try it at home.)

Audiences want to know and be moved by what you are singing about. Using dynamics will help your audience stay more focused on you. Here's another example. Can you imagine watching a movie that is only one camera shot, spoken by only one actor in exactly the same manner for a long time? You probably wouldn't pay much attention past a minute or so. The same can be said for a "boring" public speaker who drones on and on in a monotone voice. Dynamics give our speech and singing presence, shape, and meaning.

When a performer belts his or her way through every song, after a while, it begins to sound like shouting. When every song we sing is pushed, up-tempo, over-the-top, high-octane, it creates the opposite effect of being exciting. It becomes numbing.

> *"When every song we sing is pushed, up-tempo, over-the-top, high-octane, it creates the opposite effect of being exciting. It becomes numbing."*

The health of the voice is also maintained more easily when belting is an option, rather than the only go-to way to sing a song. Too much belting is usually exhausting for the singer, as well as for the audience. By pairing this high-octane singing with more subtle approaches, we create texture, balance, and artistry.

When Should I Use Belting?

That said, some songs simply need to be powerful. Loud. Excited. Full-throttle. Some songs have to be belted out for heightened drama and energy, or they just don't sound right. During passionate high moments of the song, a singer can be loud and emotionally animated. A well-composed musical arrangement helps to build the song, too. It supports the singer by conveying the song's meaning with instrumental choices and dynamics. A few examples of this kind of song are Jennifer Hudson's stunning rendition of "And I Am Telling You I'm Not Going" from *Dreamgirls*, "Firework" sung by Katy Perry, "Greatest Love of All" sung by the late Whitney Houston, "Dream On" by Aerosmith, and "On My Own" from the popular musical *Les Misérables*. When singing in a blues or rock style, a brief but loud, even aggressive-sounding moment may be just right. Musical theater styles commonly use belting at peak moments; in a theatrical setting, belting can heighten a comedic scene, intensify energy, or portray a character's quest to conquer a challenge. Even though these songs are decidedly "big," they still have ebbs and flows including soft portions, using the rise and fall of dynamics for dramatic effect and expressive musicianship.

When Should I Avoid Belting?

Besides the artistic value of using belting judiciously as a tool, there are distinct physical reasons to avoid belting. Discussed in depth in chapters 2 and 3, these reasons include maintaining your vocal health and honoring the physical structures of the voice you were born with.

KNOW THYSELF: LEARN YOUR NEUTRAL VOICE, YOUR HEALTHY VOICE, YOUR TIRED VOICE

When you sing, it is very important to know your top-to-bottom vocal range as well as the extent of your physical ability. One useful gauge for this is familiarity with your "neutral" voice when you are not belting.

What Is My Neutral or "Natural" Voice?

Your neutral voice is neither loud nor soft. It is comfortable to sing in, and does not tire easily. A healthy neutral voice is fairly clean-sounding, without additional raspiness or breathiness.[1] The make-up of your neutral or "natural" voice has a great deal to do with how you use it regularly. To discover what your neutral voice is, first consider: is your everyday speaking voice loud, moderate, or soft? Do people ask you to repeat yourself when you speak, or to tone it down a little?

---

1. Two exceptions to this guideline are: if your natural voice is *always* raspy or breathy, or if it is generally difficult for you to speak. If either of these describe you, it is important to see a *laryngologist*—a medical doctor who specializes in treating the voice. This doctor can look at your voice with a scope to learn precisely what is going on physically in your larynx. Please see "What Is Vocal Fry?" in chapter 2, and chapter 4, for more information.

For women, do you sing most comfortably in your higher voice or your lower voice? For men, do you sing in falsetto when you're humming a tune casually or in your lower full voice? If your voice is naturally loud, belting may come easily. If it is naturally softer, belting may be more difficult to access.

Becoming Vocally Flexible and Agile

Your voice is a highly flexible instrument that travels through high and low pitches all day long when you speak, usually without your awareness. When you speak, you usually focus on what you want to *say*, instead of noticing how your voice moves and sounds. Your "natural" voice has a range of timbres and colors that you can learn to use intentionally when you speak or sing. It fluctuates to add emphasis to what you're saying. Your "natural vocal type" lies within that general range.

Some teachers, especially those from more traditional teaching methods, will tell you where in your range you should be singing, and what "type" (quality) of voice you have. This has as much to do with the aesthetics of certain styles of music, and how your vocal timbre and colors work within those styles, as it does with your vocal anatomy. For popular music styles, expression and emotional range become most important, rather than staying within the parameters of a described vocal type.

No one can produce every singing tone we hear someone else do. Just as our bodies come in many shapes and sizes, so do our voices. A flute cannot be a bass clarinet and will never sound like one, though notes overlap within their ranges. A female soprano singing an E4 (above middle C) will sound very different than a male tenor singing that exact pitch. There is no "you should be singing in this part of your voice" rule that can be described in a book, because each person uses his or her voice differently. Speaking is incredibly malleable, blending dozens of factors such as where you grew up, your family dynamics, your native language, your high school, your personality; even the background sounds in your hometown affect how you learned to speak. You may be a person who communicates using a different part of your range from where you typically sing. Or, you may speak with the familiar, slightly gravelly *vocal fry* speech pattern that, unfortunately, tires easily (please see "What Is Vocal Fry?" in chapter 2). All of these factors impact whether or not belting will come easily to you and without straining.

Your Healthy Voice and Range

Become familiar with your voice. Learn what range of notes you sing in most comfortably, naturally. Know your top and bottom notes by name and the edges of your range. Know where in the middle area of your range your voice tends to be less reliable, or thinner. (Everyone has a spot or two. This is totally normal.) Know when your voice tends to get tired, and when it is supple and flexible. Know thyself. This will not limit you, but guide you. Learn how softly and loudly you can sing every pitch without strain. You test these things by singing, while keeping a detailed daily journal of your progress. A weeklong view of your practice, especially when coupled with videotaping yourself singing, provides an excellent gauge of your vocal range and health. A sample journal is provided for you to use in chapter 4.

HOW DID BELTING DEVELOP?

Being able to produce a strong sound is a natural part of the human voice. Utilizing a loud voice is a basic part of communication, such as warning someone who appears to be in danger. If you yell, "Hey, you, LOOK OUT!!" you use many of the same anatomical parts of your voice that you use when you belt. When, then, did this loud voice become a fashionable way to sing?

Across the span of human history, artistic musical styles have developed and changed along with aesthetic views on what is good or bad singing. Our aesthetic preferences are heavily influenced by the people we admire, by our culture, and by the expressed views of others. People living all around the globe sing with wide-ranging musical characteristics, ornamentations, and timbres, including singing in the strong manner we call belting. In contrast, Western European "classical" bel canto singing—originating in Italy and now frequently the norm in formal vocal training—stresses highly refined, "beautiful" legato lines and tones. (Though what *beauty* is depends upon the subjective ear of the listener. It's just like fashion trends. "You're wearing *that*?!") Belting is typically not embraced by a bel canto approach.

What is described as "popular singing" changes as frequently as clothing fashions. In the 1950s and 1960s, for instance, many of the most popular singers were "crooners" with melodious, soothing voices that inspired fans to fall in love with them. Artists including Frank Sinatra, Rosemary Clooney, Nat King Cole, Sammy Davis Jr., Ella Fitzgerald, and Pat Boone are in this category; even many of the rocker Elvis Presley's songs were sweet and melodic.

Today, popular music reveals musical influences from all around the world that are blended together, making it increasingly difficult to separate styles and cultures. American musical styles, such as rock, blues, jazz, and R&B, share a unique cross-pollination of multicultural roots derived from its social history including European, African, and even Native American influences. If you travel to West Africa, you'll hear a belted sound in traditional call-response songs accompanied by drumming. Field hollers (also called "field calls"), which were songs from farming and other forms of hard work that are associated with African American spirituals, became an integral component of American blues singing. Although most recordings of field hollers are hard to find, here are some examples of this kind of early singing that (currently) can be found online.

1. Annie Grace Horn Dodson's "Field Call," which is sung in a plaintive voice without words, bending notes to express strong feelings. Visit folkways.si.edu to find this recording.

2. Alan Lomax's recording of "No More, My Lawd" sung by African American chain-gang inmates c. 1933.

3. Alan Lomax's recording of the chain-gang singing "Early in the Mornin'."

4. "Worry Blues," part of a collection of recordings made by John and Ruby Lomax in 1939 on their *Southern States Recording Trip.* (Performers: W.S. Harrison, "Jaybird"; Sylvester Jones, "Texas Stavin' Chain"; and Wallace Chains, "Stavin' Chains"). Visit memory.loc.gov to find this recording.

5. More recent examples that carry on the tradition are Nina Simone singing "Work Song," and Harry Belafonte singing "Banana Boat Song (Day O)."

Other traditional regional music uses a belt voice, such as Appalachian mountain singing (Sacred Harp), where singers shout their songs together in four-part (or more) joyous abandon. Even some operatic singing requires a belted voice (though it is not often called that), such as nineteenth-century operas that became increasingly dramatic and loud, requiring the singer to be heard over full and dense orchestral arrangements. (However, this powerful singing approach is not generally taught until the vocal student is advanced, for fear of damaging the voice.)

The blues form, with its raw, expressive, melismatic vocal approach (a melisma is a phrase with notes that bend and blend together), is at the core of American popular music. Mid-twentieth century musical theater has also had a big influence on how we belt today. In those days, there were no microphones to boost singing volume above an orchestra. Projecting a voice depended upon the singer's lungpower, timbre, and diction. One of the earliest "belting" stars was Ethel Merman (1908–1984), dubbed "the first lady of the musical comedy stage," who began to gain notice in 1930 in the musical *Girl Crazy*. Though never a trained singer, her captivating performances and brassy, strong mezzo-soprano voice brought her great notoriety, changing musical theater forever. Pressing the female voice high into the middle range, without concern for a beautiful tone or delicateness, became a hallmark of what we think of today as belting.

Judy Garland (*The Wizard of Oz*, 1939; *Meet Me in St. Louis*, 1944) was also a celebrated belter, as is her daughter Liza Minnelli (*Cabaret*, 1972). Barbra Streisand's many notable performances brought such recognition to belting that for a time, everyone wanted to sing just like her, and she forever influenced popular singing to follow (e.g., *Funny Girl*, 1968; *A Star Is Born*, 1976). All three of these women are extraordinary artists who set the bar extremely high. To hear an example of Ethel Merman, Judy Garland, and Barbra Streisand singing together, watch their 1963 television clip on *The Judy Garland Show*. For another, in 1963, Judy and Barbra also performed a televised medley together, blending their belting styles with relaxed, fun, and conversational singing that is very engaging. These clips are both currently available on YouTube.

As popular music in the later part of the twentieth century evolved, smooth popular singing gave way to gritty styles such as rock, Motown, and gospel music, drawing in audiences with strong expressions of emotion and spirit. Gospel groups are often loud and passionate, raising voices together in praise of the holy. Rock singers traditionally belt out tunes to create powerful, raw performances, while early rock singers—including Elvis Presley—borrowed a great deal of stylistic grit and power from popular African American R&B[2] singers like Big Joe Turner and Fats Domino. The always-in-demand gritty sound of rock singing is, unfortunately, often caused by vocal overuse and strain, plus bad health habits such as smoking, drug use, and heavy drinking. Many of us have come to love the sound of a gritty voice, but singing in this way too often comes at a cost to the body including serious vocal damage. (For more on healthier ways to sing gritty styles such as rock, please see chapters 3 and 5.)

---

2 The term "rhythm and blues," or R&B, was coined in 1948 by Billboard's Jerry Wexler, replacing the offensive term "race music" for popular black artists of the day. In 1969, *Billboard* replaced the term with "Best Selling Soul Singles."

BELTING IS NOT FOR EVERYONE

Artistically speaking, there are hundreds of artists who prefer to sing in a conversational or more relaxed way, using less vocal propulsion than is needed to belt. Artists such as Norah Jones, James Taylor, Alison Krauss, Roy Orbison, Emmylou Harris, Diana Krall, Colbie Caillat, Sade, and Paul Simon are but a few examples of expressive singers who don't push their voices hard. Then, there are a few revered vocalists who use belt singing from time to time, but don't rely on it in order to put a song across: Luther Vandross, Roberta Flack, Mel Tormé, Bobby McFerrin, Ella Fitzgerald, Frank Sinatra, India Arie, Kurt Elling, and Donny Hathaway. Stylistically, there are several genres of music for which singers rarely belt, two examples being contemporary folk music and several forms of jazz.

If you believe you need to belt in order to be "good enough to make it" in today's market, reconsider that belief. Belting is a tool, and it can be very powerful. But plenty of today's artists are extremely popular and effective without pushing their voices hard all the time. True, if you are focused on pop styles, belting may be a featured part of your toolkit. Just be sure that's the sound you *really* want to use. Be sure to view the videos referenced in this book. They present recorded examples of belting so you can observe the differences between effective and strained belting, differences between male and female singers, as well as exercises for you to practice for improving how you belt.

Before we get to the exercises, let's take a look at what happens in your body when you sing, so that as you practice you have a clear mental picture of your vocal instrument. This will help you to get the results you want.

CHAPTER 2

The Vocal Anatomy of Belting

When you have an accurate picture of the general shifts and movements in your voice, you can learn to monitor what is happening while you sing. Singing technique teaches you to save energy and stress on the voice by releasing contractions in muscles that are not in use at the moment, while engaging the muscles you need. This is especially important for healthy belting. Knowing what areas to relax and what areas to activate is essential in order for your voice to last.

Whenever you do something physical, your body responds largely to how you *believe* you move. If you conceive the movements of your voice inaccurately when you belt, muscles will contract that are not needed for smooth and flexible vocal technique. If you think high notes are literally "up," for example, you might unconsciously tend to crane your neck and tense your body when you sing them, as if to compensate for gravity. The result is not only unnecessary tension, but also typically a sound that just isn't working well. Too often, vocal fatigue or even injury will result from over-contracting muscles unnecessarily.

Let's take a closer look at what happens when you belt, to correct any misunderstandings or confusion. This will provide you with a map to guide you most effectively through your belting practice and performing.

THREE PARTS OF YOUR BODY THAT WORK TOGETHER

Vocal production of any kind has three main components that work in coordination with each other: air source, tone generator, and resonating spaces. Belting is a form of singing. It uses the same body parts as any other type of singing.

In order to sing or speak, you need air. All day long, your lungs take in air and expel it, acting as a kind of bellows. When you sing or speak, this inhaled air creates pressure in your lungs that is then released up and out through your larynx ("voice box"), enabling your vocal folds to vibrate together. This vibration produces tone. There are muscles and cartilages within your larynx that move continuously, helping to create the tone. Then, the tone is shaped in the spaces of your mouth, pharynx, and sinuses, especially by the movement of your tongue.

All of this happens as you listen back to yourself while you sing, guiding yourself with thoughts (and judgments… "Did I really just sound as bad as I think? How embarrassing!" or, "Wow, that note I just belted was freakin' *awesome!*"). Singing is a constant feedback loop between your thoughts and your body: expectation, action, creating sound, judging the results, and making adjustments. Sometimes, you may even make judgments and adjustments before you sing a single note!

Figure 2.1 illustrates a typical mental process that affects how you sing. First, you think about how you want to sound. Then, you take in air and begin to sing, producing sound. While you sing, you listen to the sound, deciding if it is what you were going for. (At this point, you might actually question yourself, halt in embarrassment, even apologize. It happens all the time in voice lessons.) Next, you make adjustments to the sound, while you are singing. Now you're back to the beginning of the cycle, planning how you want to sound and hoping it will come out all right. If you were unhappy with how you just sang, your breathing will be affected in the next go-round (usually, it becomes shallower), and your throat may constrict as your body tries to protect you from making another error. Or, your belting may be pushed out with more force to compensate for your perception of how you sound. If you were pleased with how you just sang, you will relax a little, and your thoughts will become less judgmental. Seem familiar?

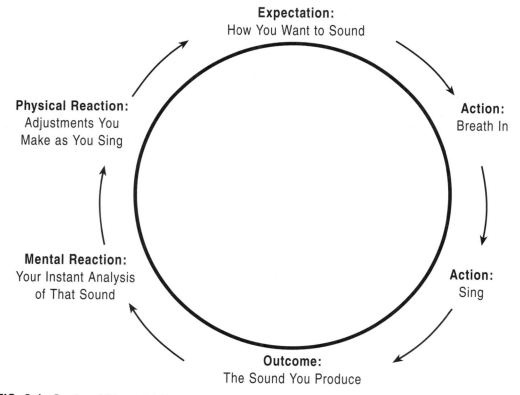

FIG. 2.1. Cycle of Thought Processes while Singing

If you aren't pleased with your belting and the cycle is consistently negative, your body will be consistently tense. How, then, can you adjust your results?

1. Study with a superb teacher who can guide you through shifting your patterns.

2. Practice. Regularly. Practice your technique, not just songs.

3. Be kind to yourself. Rome wasn't built in a day. It takes, on average, twenty-one days for the body to change a habit, and that's assuming you replace that habit with a different behavior that you practice daily.

4. Record yourself. Did you judge how you sounded fairly? Did you like the tone of your belt voice? Maybe it wasn't so bad! And, you can hear and see truthfully what you need to work on.

AIR: THE SOURCE OF YOUR BELTING POWER

Your voice is a wind instrument. When you study singing technique, you learn to manage your breathing in order to make singing more effective while minimizing wear and tear on the body. Air can and should do most of the work for you. It is the source, the power of your voice. By learning to inhale lower in your torso and to keep air inside you longer—which increases air pressure in your lungs—it becomes easier to sing each phrase intentionally. This is because when the air you exhale passes up and out through your vocal folds, it actually helps to suck them together in vibration. For optimum singing technique, you coordinate this exhalation with a *resistance* response at the site of your vocal folds (so the air doesn't leak out there).

This is how it works. When you breathe in, muscles in your larynx open a passageway into your *trachea* (windpipe), air is sucked into your lungs, and the air pressure there increases. Then, as you release the air when you sing, the pressure drops as the air stream zips over the rounded edges of the vocal folds. This helps to pull the vocal folds together through a process called the *Bernoulli Effect*[3], and the folds close. Then, air pressure builds up again, which separates the folds again. All of this happens extremely rapidly in a continuous wave-like cycle, where little puffs of air are produced by this action at your larynx, *hundreds* of times a second. When you hold your breath, the passageway to your lungs is sealed tight. This seal is at the site of your vocal folds. (Try it: you cannot hold your breath and sing at the same time.)

---

3. Named after 18th century Swiss scientist Daniel Bernoulli, this same air pressure effect sucks the shower curtain into your hot shower on a cold day, and also helps to lift airplanes.

You can do a quick experiment to see how airflow works in your voice. Take two pieces of paper and hold them about an inch apart. Blow in between them. What will happen? Will they separate as you blow? In fact, you'll see that the opposite happens. When you blow in between the two papers, they are sucked together. The shifts in air pressure cause this suction. This is also precisely what happens in your voice to bring your vocal folds together in vibration. Then, your pitch is altered because of a complex shifting of muscles, cartilages, and ligaments in your larynx, controlled by your thoughts. These movements are discussed later in "Larynx: Your Tone Generator."

If you are nervous or anxious when you sing, your body receives a general message that you may be at risk. This is fear. Fear creates important self-defense reactions in the body, but these reactions make singing much harder. The muscles in and around the larynx constrict, which is your body's way of protecting you from any potential harm to your breathing. Obviously, when you sing, you are not at risk for drowning or suffocating, but a human being's primal fear of not having adequate air for staying alive will trump any attempt to sing. Therefore, part of training singers to breathe more effectively is to *relax*, rather than contract, the over-zealous muscles in your throat that can cause unnecessary tension and make singing much harder. In chapter 4, we'll look at techniques for managing nerves and anxiety when you sing.

Diaphragm Muscle

The ever-moving, large, and often-cited *diaphragm* muscle, located beneath your lungs and heart, facilitates each and every breath you take in. Shaped like a parachute, your diaphragm muscle is connected all along the base of your ribs and anchored to your lumbar spine. It separates your heart and lungs from all of the other organs in your torso. The diaphragm is the muscle that is responsible for about 70 percent of your breathing.

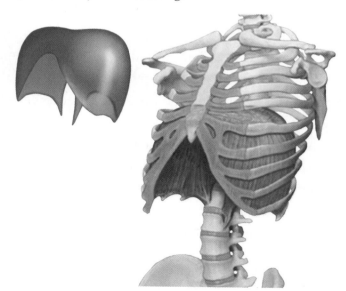

FIG. 2.2. Diaphragm Muscle. On exhalation, the diaphragm muscle relaxes into the upward position illustrated here. On inhalation, it contracts to pull downward, creating space in your chest that allows your lungs to fill with air.

Belters are told frequently to breathe or sing "from your diaphragm." What does this mean exactly? Your diaphragm muscle contracts to move downward every time you breathe in, and it relaxes to its upward position every time you exhale. It does this throughout your life, *every* minute of every day, until you take your last breath. For this reason, you always "breathe from (the action of) your diaphragm"! Since the diaphragm is a muscle, not a lung, technically you cannot breathe from it any more than you can breathe from the *intercostal* muscles in between your ribs, which also move when you inhale and exhale.

You control the release of your air with slight upper abdominal contractions and by using the intercostal muscles in between your ribs. These actions assist your diaphragm in releasing more gradually as you exhale, helping to maintain the air pressure you need for singing. These coordinated movements support your belting significantly. Thus, the power generator for belting is the air you breathe.

TIP: Breathing for Belting Is About Coordination, Not Super Abdominal Strength

Breathing coordination does not require extraordinary strength. It does not require you to squeeze your stomach or tighten any muscle excessively. It is, instead, a coordination of balance. You breathe in, slowly when possible, lower into your lungs. You pause. You relax. You trust that you will have adequate air. You release the air more slowly than for other activities, to allow the air stream to balance the vibrations of your vocal folds, and repeat. Practices such as yoga are very beneficial for this type of breathing awareness. Sit-ups are good too, as long as you don't pull on your head and crane your neck when you do them.

Breathing Relaxation Exercise

Start by slowing down. Take in a deliberate breath, counting to four. Hold your breath. Are your muscles tight? Or does it feel more like you have simply paused a breath cycle? Listen to your thoughts. Are they racing... or slowing into peacefulness? Now, release your air to a count of 16, listening to the sound as it hisses out between your teeth and tongue. This is similar to the sensation of breath management: you take in air and control how you release it. Keep yourself in a peaceful, slower state. Supported breathing for singing does not require intense muscle contractions.

See "Breath Management" in chapter 3, and also part II for more breathing exercises.

LARYNX: YOUR TONE GENERATOR

As we've seen, when you sing, air leaving your lungs passes up through the delicate vocal membranes within your larynx, causing the vocal folds to vibrate together on each puff. This is what produces an initial tone. The tone's pitch and volume are affected by a complex array of muscles, ligaments, and cartilages within your larynx. There are nine cartilages in your larynx:

- three single ones: the large and shield-shaped *thyroid cartilage*, the ringed *cricoid cartilage*, and the leaf-shaped *epiglottic cartilage* that helps you to swallow

- three paired cartilage groups: *arytenoid*, *corniculate*, and *cuneiform*

The movements within your larynx for singing (and speaking) are controlled by your thoughts, both conscious and unconscious.

Within this complex array are two primary laryngeal muscle groups we refer to most often in voice lessons. When you sing lower notes, a muscle group called the *TA* contracts. The TA muscles, named for the *thyroid* and *arytenoid* cartilages they are attached to, pull your vocal edges together and *thicken* their area of contact. They also shorten your vocal folds to lower pitch. The TAs are hard at work when you sing in "chest" voice. They are also very active when you belt. Then, when you sing higher notes, the *CT muscles*, named for the *cricoid* and *thyroid* cartilages they are attached to, contract to pull your large thyroid cartilage forward and slightly down. This causes your vocal folds to stretch longer and thinner, raising pitch.

TA *Thyroarytenoid* muscles, named for the *thyroid* and *arytenoid* cartilages the muscles attach to inside your larynx. The *vocalis* muscle, often referred to by singing books, is located within the TAs. It is part of the same complex muscle group. Contractions of the TA lower pitch and thicken the area where your vocal folds meet in vibration. This is what happens when you sing in "chest voice."

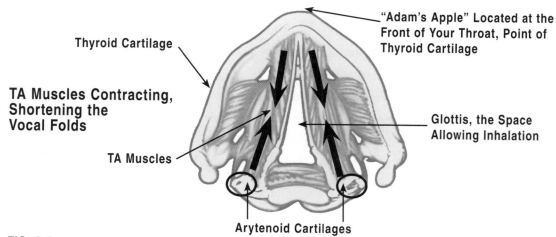

FIG. 2.3. Vocal Mechanism. Inside view of the TAs at work, looking down at the vocal folds, seen from above through the mouth.

CT *Cricothyroid* muscles, named for the *thyroid* and *cricoid* cartilages the muscles attach to. The CT contractions lengthen and thin your vocal folds, raising pitch.

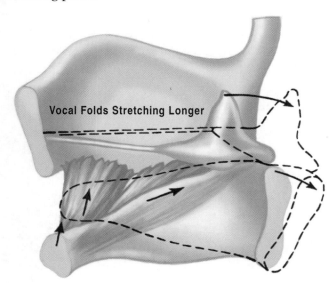

FIG. 2.4. CT Muscles Stretching Vocal Folds Forward for Higher notes. CT muscles contract inside the larynx to pull the thyroid cartilage forward, which raises pitch.

The movements of the TA and CT are in a constant, normal state of useful antagonism. However, with the TA contraction pressing your vocal folds together, and with the CT contraction lengthening and thinning them, your voice can move only so far in these two opposing directions before it reaches its flexibility limit. That point is what we sometimes call a "break." You have probably experienced a break when you belt, especially if you push up your chest voice. A person with a flexible singing approach travels through these movements with practiced coordination, allowing the TA and CT muscles to move freely depending upon the sound the singer is after. (See "Why You Don't Have to 'Break'" on page 27.)

Singers often mistakenly believe that muscles in the voice somehow cause the vocal folds to vibrate together. Belters, especially, often mistakenly believe you can beef up more vocal muscle to improve your sound and stamina. The truth is, the vibrations are so fast that this wouldn't be possible. When you sing the pitch A4 (440 Hz), for example—just a sixth above middle C—your vocal folds vibrate together at a remarkable 440 times per second! (It would be like squeezing your lips tightly together to make a motorboat sound—just won't work.)

Laryngeal movements can be so seamless, especially after years of singing, that they become second nature and even unnoticeable. These movements are constant. It is also important to observe that you may *feel* movements in your larynx that are not audible to others. You will most likely *hear* your tone change more than others do. This is because you hear the sound of your voice from both inside and outside your head.

FACE, NECK, AND MOUTH: YOUR RESONATORS

Once the tone is created in the larynx, it picks up resonance in the vocal tract. The vocal tract is made of the spaces and housing above and around your *pharynx* (the back of your throat and sinuses).

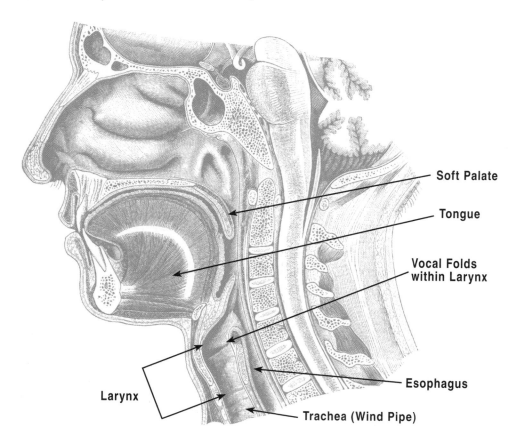

Soft Palate

Tongue

Vocal Folds within Larynx

Esophagus

Larynx

Trachea (Wind Pipe)

FIG. 2.5. Overview of Vocal Tract (with Mouth Closed)

While the laryngeal cartilages move and pivot to create pitch and tone, the entire larynx also lowers or rises to assist in adjusting pitch and resonance. In this way, the voice functions something like the slide of a trombone.

Your singing tone is created by how you shape vowels in your mouth. Your tongue, the structure that is most involved with the actual timbre of your voice, creates these vowels. Even a small adjustment in the shape of the tongue can change a vowel sound, affecting *overtones* produced in the vocal tract. When the mouth is closed as in figure 2.5, not enough resonant space exists for tone to resonate effectively, which makes a belt sound very difficult to produce. Overtones—the series of frequencies that are above the fundamental pitch, and combine with it to give a note its quality—furnish your voice with its presence and tone. For singers, overtones change noticeably depending on how you shape a vowel when your mouth is open (mostly on the inside). The way you pronounce your vowels varies depending on where you're from (your first language and regional accent), how much tension is in your tongue, and on how you were taught to sing. We spend a great deal of time in voice lessons adjusting vowels and relearning how to pronounce them for singing, which is different from speaking. Voice teachers do not always agree on how to produce vowels "correctly," or even which tones are the most aesthetically pleasing! (This varies greatly depending on the style in which you are singing. For example, bel canto training—in which you rarely if ever belt—stresses Italian vowel pronunciations for a very even, balanced tonal palette, whereas contemporary vowels are often bright and broad.)

WHAT'S THE BEST WAY TO GET LOUDER?

In order to belt, we must be loud. To sing loudly, we use *resonance* to amplify the tones that are produced within the larynx. There is a great deal of confusion about how to do this, including what parts of the body vibrate or resonate. *Resonance* and *vibration* are two different things. Let's understand the differences.

Resonance and Vibration

Sound is created by air molecules that move and bounce against surfaces, detected by our ears and interpreted by our brains. For any sound to be amplified, there must be resonance. Resonance occurs when molecules of sound bounce around within a space. Vibration, on the other hand, occurs when an object oscillates, such as a plucked guitar string. Your vocal folds *vibrate*. Your chest *vibrates*. But the spaces in your mouth, pharynx, and sometimes your nasal cavity, *resonate* when you sing or speak. There are no resonant spaces in your head or chest. Therefore, in spite of the familiar term "chest voice," your voice does not reside in your chest. The same is true for "head voice," which is not located in your forehead or brain. "Chest voice" and "head voice" are common—though often confusing—terms for singing registers that are produced by complex and coordinated muscle movements in the vocal tract. [See "Understanding Vocal Registers" later in this chapter.]

> *"In spite of the familiar term 'chest voice,' your voice does not reside in your chest! The same is true for 'head voice,' which is not located in your forehead or brain."*

Adjusting Your Tone

Forward, dark, nasal, round, bright—these are terms often used to describe vowel shape or "placement" in the mouth that affect the tone of your voice. You adjust these resonant spaces in your vocal tract all day long when you speak and when you sing. If your sound is nasal or *twangy*, the soft palate at the back of your throat is not fully lifted, allowing air to pass through your sinuses. This allows air to resonate in your mouth and nose at the same time, creating a nasal quality. When your sound is *dark*, the space in the back of your throat is enlarged and the sound is focused there. A *forward* sound often seems like it is coming from the front of your face in the "mask" area. *Round* and *bright* tones describe shaping the inside of the mouth to change the balance of overtones produced there, which affects how you sound.

Tone Exercise

You can discover these tones and their placement in the mouth by experimentation. You'll need pen and paper. To measure your volume accurately, you can use a simple recording device that shows you a volume meter, such as GarageBand or a smart phone app.

1. Start by holding a note in the middle of your range, singing an "Ah" vowel, as in the phrase "P<u>a</u>k the C<u>ah</u> in H<u>ah</u>vad Y<u>ah</u>d." Write down what it feels like when you hold the vowel. Write down what it sounds like. Is any area feeling tight, or is the note relaxed? Can you feel vibrations anywhere in your vocal tract? Is the sound breathy, or clean? How loudly can you sing the note? Keep track of how many counts you can sing the note before you need to get a new breath. Keep track of your volume with the meter.

2. Now, change the vowel to "Aw," as in "<u>Aw</u>, what an <u>awe</u>some dog I <u>saw</u> at the <u>mall</u>!" Write down what this vowel feels like and sounds like. Have the sensations changed from when you sang the "Ah" vowel? Can you hold the note for more counts? Can you sing this vowel more loudly? Or does "Ah" work better for you?

3. Repeat the process, this time singing an "Ee" vowel as in, "S<u>ee</u> thr<u>ee</u> tr<u>ees</u> in the br<u>eeze</u>." Write down how singing a note on "Ee" feels and sounds, and how many counts you can hold it for. Did changing the vowel to "Ee" make your throat feel tighter, or more relaxed? Can you sing the sound louder than "Ah" and "Aw," or is it softer?

4. Repeat the sequence for all three vowels on a higher pitch, again taking notes and measuring your volume. Notice what changes (or stays the same).

5. Finally, repeat the sequence focusing the sound in the front of your mouth, behind your front teeth where the bony hard palate is. We sometimes call this "forward placement."

Each of us produces sound slightly differently. By learning what happens inside your mouth on simple vowel shapes while holding one note, you begin to learn how to focus the sound in different areas of your mouth and face. This ability to focus your sound is an important tool in vocal technique.

Some languages and regional accents are spoken more forward or back in the mouth, affecting singing technique and sound. A slightly twangy sound can be useful for belting, and to color some styles such as country music, though it is undesirable in classical singing. Generally, belting uses a forward placement, which makes the sound very bright, not round or dark.

Keep in mind that these terms are very subjective and may convey different meanings to different people. These are guidelines, not absolutes. Each person produces a tone based on how he or she understands the goal, including slight differences in mouth shapes. The bottom line is the outcome. If the produced sound works and your voice is not tense, then the tone is working for you.

UNDERSTANDING VOCAL REGISTERS

The term *registers* is used to convey several meanings, depending upon context. Register sometimes means the overall vocal range in which your voice is most naturally resonant and free. For instance, are you a counter tenor, tenor, baritone, bass, soprano, mezzo-soprano, contralto (alto), or coloratura? Registration can also reference a requirement in operatic or musical theater literature, such as a role that is written specifically for a mezzo-soprano or bass-baritone. For wind players, whose instruments are similar in some ways to the human voice, registration refers to how air is blown through the instrument to shift octaves.

In vocal instruction, the term "registers" frequently references several distinct-sounding qualities of your singing voice (though belting is not on this list). This can be confusing because vocal teachers and reference texts don't necessarily mean precisely the same thing when they use these terms. Moreover, if you focus on singing from the register you think you should be using, you are going to limit your vocal flexibility.

Nonetheless, because registers are so commonly described in vocal instruction, let's clarify the terms here, for our purposes. There are five register areas consistently cited in vocal instruction: *head voice, chest voice, falsetto, whistle tone,* and *fry voice.* Are you singing in a light, thin tone? That is often head voice. Is your sound loud, full, and low? That is often chest voice. For men, is your sound high in your range and very light? That is likely falsetto. Described in the next few pages, these terms label a range of notes that are each produced with a fairly consistent and uniform quality, regardless of your vocal "type."

Which register should you use when you belt? That is a frequent but misguided question. Why? Belting is not a register! Belting is a *quality*. It means you are singing loudly. The truth is, it is impossible to describe *exactly* how you are using your voice, especially from the pages of a book. Each person uses his or her voice differently. Sometimes, it is even difficult for the voice teacher in a lesson to determine precisely what parts of your vocal tract are in use. Because of the complexity of the vocal process, voice teachers will often use generalized terms to guide you toward a desired result. For example, your teacher may instruct you to "sing in your head voice" or to "use your mix voice," hoping the direction will help you make a shift in how you're singing.

Don't worry about what register you are using when you belt. This will free you up to *sing*. You are not dialing up your sound to belt as if you have a built-in remote control! Read on.

Wait, WHAT? *Two* Registers, That's It?

There is even more to our story. As recent advances in vocal science help us to learn more about what happens internally when we sing, we now understand that the human voice has really just *two* usable registers. Yes, really! This means the many parts within your larynx move through two primary physical orientations when you sing. These are typically called *chest voice* or *full voice*, which is TA-dominant, and *head voice* or *lighter voice*, which is CT-dominant. Most of the time when we sing, these two registers work together, as described earlier, as a cooperation between the CT and TA muscles (see "Larynx: Your Tone Generator"). *Other registers result from variations in how these muscles respond together.* Understanding the voice as a blend of these two highly flexible functions is a much easier, and more accurate, way of perceiving how the vocal mechanism moves throughout all of your range and qualities. This is why focusing on your registration when you belt just causes confusion—or worse—vocal fatigue and strain. Understanding your voice as two *inter*dependent registers is also more flexible than believing your voice has a series of settings (like switches, or springs that pop and snap). It opens up many more possibilities for a reliable and sustainable belt voice.

Judging How You Sound

Your voice can produce a wide variety of sounds, many of which are traditionally rejected aesthetically for singing. When we are children, we are unconscious of using our voices in a colorful way. The voice naturally traverses the two usable registers all day long—blending, softening, contracting, going high or low, becoming softer or louder, sounding thin or strident. When we get older, we become self-conscious of how we believe we sound to others, and begin to limit the tones we produce. We learn instead to edit ourselves, to judge ourselves. You may think, "I hate hearing myself on a recording!" or, "I want to sound more like that singer I love." We are pretty hard on ourselves, and in my opinion, singers are often wrong about how they sound. Agreed, not *every* human sound is beauty to the ears. (I'm picturing some pretty gross sounds as I write this, like snoring and clearing the throat.) And as we have seen, what is beautiful is truly in the ear of the beholder. When we belt, vocal beauty per se is not usually the goal. A strident tone—which would be flat-out rejected in many vocal studios— can help to convey power, to be expressive. Belting can be enhanced by tones that may sound terrible in a spoken voice, or be rejected by other singing styles. There are plenty of well-known belting singers who may be very pleasing to look at, but whose voices are not beautiful in a traditional sense. It doesn't matter. Do you love their songs? The rhythms? The messages? Their confidence? Perhaps these things are what you find intoxicating!

Here is a challenge to help you free yourself from a too-limiting judgment about how you sound. Can you imitate a cat? A horse? A pig? A cow? Every first-grader has learned these simple sounds. Listen to yourself as you go through the range of barnyard voices. Your own voice becomes low or high, squeaky and thin, or fat and resonant. Does this seem too silly? How about attempting to imitate someone speaking with a thick accent? Or, the voice of a child, the voice of a tired person, or of someone who just won the lottery? In all of these examples, you have made shifts in your mouth, with your tongue, and with your laryngeal muscles. In each case, you also need air to produce these sounds. The more willing you are to free yourself of judgment, at least while you are experimenting, the more free your vocal palette will be to produce sounds that make belting effortless.

When you sing you can activate a wider range of timbres, colors, and tones than you probably use for everyday speaking, reaching high and low as your vocal mechanism contracts, releases, stretches, tightens, vibrates, and shakes. Within this wide range of options, the TA and CT muscles are doing most of the work. Let's return to our discussion of these muscles.

What Is Chest Voice?

The sensation you feel in your chest when you sing low notes is the vibration of solid parts of your chest, such as ribs and lung tissue. Although there is always air in your lungs, your voice does not resonate there with any usable effect, because your lungs sit well below your voice. Instead, what we call "chest voice" happens when the TA muscle contracts to press the membranes of the vocal folds together in vibration across a thickened area of contact, while air is pushed up against them from beneath. To sing low in your range, you need this thicker area of contact and increased air pressure in order to make any kind of usable sound. (The exception is when you sing into a microphone, enabling you to sing extremely softly. See chapter 3 for a discussion of microphone technique.) As you ascend in pitch (activating the CT movement, which stretches, thins, and lengthens your vocal folds), the TA muscle stays in contraction in chest voice, in an opposing direction to the CT's movement. If you don't let the TA lessen its contraction as you ascend in pitch, you reach a "break" where the two opposing movements have no more ability to continue. When that happens, your voice may crack or strain; you'll realize that you just can't sing any higher without adjusting your sound. This happens commonly when singers try to stay completely in chest voice for belting. The increased pressure from this action also creates greater velocity or impact on your vocal folds when they meet in vibration. Vocal fatigue or even injury and scarring can occur with this repeated assault. (See "How Can I Belt without Harming My Voice?" in chapter 4 about healthy chest voice singing for belting, and also watch Demonstration Video 26, "Your 'Break' and Blending Registers.") However, if you sing respectfully below this threshold, using adequate breath support so that your larynx muscles don't overly contract, chest voice is a perfectly fine—and necessary—part of your singing tool kit.

26

In women with higher-toned voices (soprano), the chest voice range is often shorter than in women whose voices are deeper-toned (alto or mezzo). Some women's laryngeal structures are simply larger than average, providing a deeper voice and a wider range for chest voice. In men with higher ranges than average, the voice may be smaller or more flexible than average, allowing for a larger range of high notes and a nearly seamless passage into falsetto. (See page 25 for more on falsetto.)

What Is Head Voice?

As we have seen, unlike what the term implies, there is no actual voice in your head, besides the spaces in your mouth, sinuses, and pharynx. *Head voice* refers instead to a *sensation* of where the voice vibrates most strongly in your face when you sing higher pitches. It is a lighter way of singing in which the CT muscle thins and elongates the vocal folds as pitch rises.

Remember, high notes are not actually high! They vibrate at a faster rate than lower notes. (On the piano, high notes are to the right. Higher notes on the guitar are played closer to the bridge, and on the thinner strings.)

When you sing middle C (C4), your vocal folds vibrate together at the same speed as any instrument producing this frequency, 261.63 Hertz (Hz). The pitch A4, sitting a sixth above middle C, vibrates at 440 Hz. Jump up an octave to A5, and the vibration rate doubles to 880 Hz. When you sing very high (relative to your own anatomy), the TA muscle has released and is fully relaxed.

With each higher note your vocal folds thin as they are stretched longer by the movement of the CT muscle on the thyroid cartilage, pulling it forward and down. This is opposite to the movement that produces chest voice.

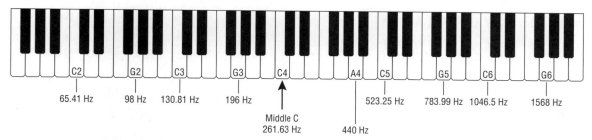

FIG. 2.6. Notes We Sing. In Hertz (Hz), shown on a keyboard.

For men, "head voice" sometimes means simply using your falsetto (again, see "What Is Falsetto?" below). The term can also mean using a mixed voice, a quality somewhere between falsetto and full voice. For women, head voice is perhaps the most widely taught register, especially for young singers (usually fourteen to twenty-four years old, or so) whose voices are less robust and usually smaller than in older women. In many vocal lessons, young women are instructed to use *only* head voice, while conversely, men are taught to push full voice up to the point of falsetto without using it. These limitations do not apply in contemporary singing. When you belt, it is uncommon to use all-head voice. It is simply too light.

What Is Falsetto? Whistle Tone?

As we've seen, when you sing very high, your TA releases, allowing your CT to stretch your vocal folds longer and thinner. In true falsetto or whistle tone the vocal folds also stiffen, creating a structure similar to that of a whistle. The vocal folds no longer meet fully in vibration, but instead, a space is created where airflow whistles through. Sometimes, the mucosal layers covering the folds also vibrate, rather than the folds themselves. Because vocal folds vibrate together in a variety of shapes and textures, falsetto (as with the other registers) does not have a one-click setting, either on or off. Although men sometimes use falsetto to imitate a woman's voice, a man's larger larynx has to adjust differently from a woman's smaller-sized voice to sing the same actual pitches (frequencies). At other times, what appears to be a man using falsetto is instead a mix voice (see page 28), with some vocal fold vibration occurring while the vocal folds are thinner and more taut.

The term "falsetto" is also sometimes used to describe a woman's head voice. However, the physical comparison to men's falsetto in women is more accurately called *whistle tone*. Whistle tone occurs when a woman's vocal edges also become thin and taut, enabling extremely high notes around G6 to G7. Examples of this sound are Mariah Carey's top-most notes produced two octaves above a song's melody, or the seemingly effortless, super-high phrases sung by the late Minnie Riperton. True falsetto is not used in belting.

What Is Mix Voice?

Mix voice is another register term that leaves room for a great deal of confusion. As we have seen, the actions of the TA and CT create two basic physical registers. Your voice is either fuller or thinner. Anything in the middle—*mix voice*—results from using TA and CT muscles together, cooperatively. This is how the majority of women sing most of the time. For men, who primarily sing in a lower voice or in falsetto for popular styles, mix voice is used less commonly, though men use mix voice to enable super-high belted notes. However, mix voice is used by many male popular and rock singers who can belt higher notes smoothly, without the thinner, reedy tone of true falsetto.

Using mix voice is the key to longevity for many demanding popular styles.

What Is Speaking Voice?

Speaking voice, also called the *modal* voice or register, occurs in the range where our hearing is best suited to understand communication. Although the overall hearing capacity for human beings ranges from about 20 to 20,000 Hz, our hearing sensitivity is the most acute for human speech, which sits around 85 to 180 Hz for an adult male, and about 165 to 255 Hz for an adult female. (For purposes of comparison, a dog can hear tones as high as 45,000 Hz, a beluga whale up to 123,000 Hz, while 3 to 4 Hz is the lowest frequency put out by elephants. The range on a piano is about 28 Hz on the bottom, up to 4,186 Hz at the top.) Our speaking voices rise and fall effortlessly throughout our day, stretching and moving parts of the vocal tract in all directions. The extreme movements to sing very high or very low notes are not typically in use for speaking. Because the range of the speaking voice is often lower-pitched than much of the range of notes we sing, the voice feels more relaxed and easy when we speak.

When boys go through puberty, the structures in the larynx grow larger rather quickly, and the thyroid cartilage shifts to lean more forward. The result is a speaking voice that is lower, and uncertain at first. The thyroid cartilage has a point that is more visible in men because of this change. We call this point the *Adam's apple*. Women also have an Adam's apple, but it is harder to see. Girls do not experience this kind of dramatic change in their voices. Instead, the voice lowers gradually over many years.

What Is Vocal Fry?

The current American style of speech often includes sounds produced by *vocal fry* (or *fry voice*): a flaccid, under-supported use of the voice. In *vocal fry* the vocal folds flap and vibrate loosely against one another, resulting in a gravelly, low-toned sound that has no recognizable pitch. Fry voice sounds as if the person just awoke from sleep or is trying to speak very quietly without whispering.

To compensate for an under-supported voice, the sphincter muscles in the throat may squeeze to help get sound out. This squeezing can cause abrasion at the vocal folds, and tires the voice more quickly. This manner of speaking is relatively recent, and hopefully will phase out soon. Be aware of speaking with fry and avoid it, to keep your singing voice healthier and more accessible. There are two exceptions to this rule:

1. Fry voice, used sparingly, can add grit to a rock vocal. When you want a little gravel in your tone, try singing with a combination of pitch and a *little* bit of fry, lower in your range so as not to strain, especially as you experiment.

2. A singer whose voice is very tense can use fry voice as an exercise approach to help loosen tense muscles.

25

To observe singing with fry voice for effect, watch Demonstration Video 25, "Fry Voice and Intentional Gravel."

WHY YOU DON'T HAVE TO "BREAK"

Your voice doesn't have to "break" when you belt! It does, however, move and pivot. Think of your voice as a system that can *transition* between different shapes when you sing.

Laryngeal structures move constantly. Every time you speak. When you swallow. Yawn. Inhale deeply. Sing low, sing medium, sing high. You do not have brittle structures in your voice that can break off. Your larynx is made of spongy, flexible areas of tissue, muscle, mucous membranes, cartilages, and ligaments that are designed to move. (This is why staying well-hydrated is so essential. Dry vocal folds will chafe.) There is no setting of clicks in your voice as on a dial. Your pharynx—the long tubal area in the back of your larynx, throat and sinuses—also contributes to the sounds you make, changing shape frequently. In figure 2.7, for example, sound moves up from the voice box through the pharynx and bounces off the hard palate (roof of the mouth). Because in figure 2.7 the soft palate is only partially lifted—meaning the airway through the sinuses is still open—sound is able to travel up and out through the back of the mouth as well as through the nose (oropharynx and nasopharynx). This creates a "twang" sound that can be bright or nasal. (Lifting the soft palate fully, as in a yawn, seals off the passageway through the sinuses, so air cannot pass through your nose. This lifting removes a twangy or nasal sound.)

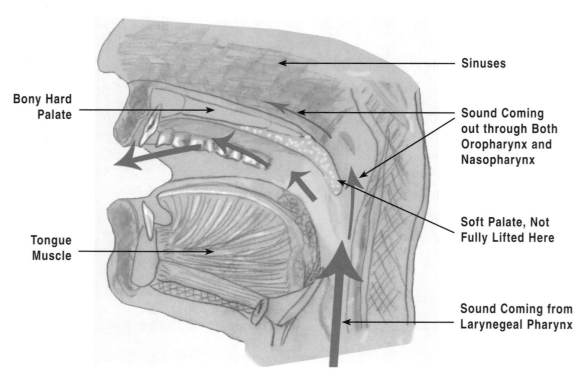

Sinuses

Bony Hard Palate

Sound Coming out through Both Oropharynx and Nasopharynx

Tongue Muscle

Soft Palate, Not Fully Lifted Here

Sound Coming from Larynegeal Pharynx

FIG. 2.7. Twang. Sound moving up from voice box through pharynx, bouncing off the hard palate (roof of mouth) and also coming out through sinuses.

There is not just one fixed location at which your voice transitions. Instead, there is a range of notes where you have options for how you may sing them. It depends upon how loudly you are singing, and on what vowel.

Using the word "break" to describe these changes suggests that if you sing in a certain way, the structures of your voice can crack apart. This belief is inaccurate. Vocal health concerns have to do with injury to the membranes themselves, or straining muscles, but there are no parts that snap at the location of a change in register.[4] Instead, use the word *transition* to describe areas where you notice your voice shifting between qualities. This term much more accurately describes the movements in your larynx. Because visualization is a useful tool for improving belting technique, using accurate language to give you a clear picture of your voice will help you to belt more freely. By saying *transition* instead of break, you can now embrace the movements, flexibility, and flow of your highly sophisticated vocal instrument.

Now that you understand the facts about how your voice actually works, let's take a look at the best approaches for belting to give you power and stamina.

---

4. Serious vocal injury such as a broken blood vessel can indeed occur on the vocal folds, but this is not what the term break refers to when describing shifts in register.

CHAPTER 3

Belting Techniques That Work

When you belt, you coordinate a blend of volume and vowel shape that creates a commanding sound. You are telling a story, expressing strong emotions and excitement through a song's melody and lyrics. You are acting, too, using more personal energy and vitality than you would during a normal spoken conversation or when singing using your "neutral" voice.

Because belting is a robust way to sing, it is very important to learn to do it well and healthfully, sustainably. "How can I possibly belt safely?" you may ask. "How can I belt night after night on the gig?" These questions send singers and voice teachers to the panic button. "NEVER belt," your teacher may warn, "You'll RUIN your voice." The truth is, when done badly, *any* kind of singing (or talking) can damage your voice. But when done well, belting is a useful asset to include in your vocal toolkit.

Let's shift this view and find the best way to belt. We will discover how your belted voice can be fully supported, stable, and flexible. You may even find that the limits that once restricted your singing are now beginning to melt away.

OBSERVE THE "LAWS OF BELTING"

This chapter guides you through the best approaches to belt singing. We'll debunk myths that create common misunderstandings about belting, and learn healthy techniques and practices that are essential for a stable, strong belting voice. As you go through this chapter, keep these important guidelines in mind:

Laws of Belting

L • Learn your limits!

A • Align your posture.

W • Warm up before you belt! Always.

S • Sing, don't scream!

of

B • Breathe.

E • Ease muscle tension.

L • Lower your jaw.

T • Trust the sound.

I • If it hurts, STOP.

N • Never strain.

G • Give yourself rest, and breaks.

FIG. 3.1. Laws of Belting

COMMON MISUNDERSTANDINGS ABOUT THE BELT VOICE

Treat it right, and your voice can be hardy and reliable for many years to come. With its origin in musical theater, belting adds an exciting element that is in high demand in contemporary styles. In today's popular music, belting is very bright, placed forward in the mouth, and sometimes twangy. Nothing like bel canto, belting is a strong way of singing and sounds harsh to some ears. Whether or not you *like* a belted vocal sound is different from claiming it is harmful to your voice. Either way, belting is but one of many tools at your disposal, and it should be respected as an option in a well-rounded, healthy vocal palette.

There are three common myths about belting that many singers and voice teachers frequently believe. These false myths reinforce concerns that belting will always hurt your voice. Let's take a look.

Myth 1: Belting Means I Always Have to Push My Voice

What does it mean to push your voice? "To push" can mean different things. In a pure sense, pushing is exerting additional force. You push a stroller. You push away sad thoughts. You push a boulder up a hill. You push a pencil across a table. As we can see, exerting force is a matter of degree. How *much* force is called for? Is using force always bad? Clearly, no, because without some force, nothing would move! A better question is, is your body overly tense, or simply active? Muscles contract to help you stand, sit, lift a bag. But they don't have to contract to their fullest potential to manage these tasks. Can you achieve the sound you want when you belt with a smaller effort than you may think? Yes, absolutely!

For starters, the idea of pushing your voice in any way may evoke self-protective concerns. "If I push my voice, I will ruin it." Your teacher may very well have told you that, too. FACT: Although you definitely do *not* want to over-stress your voice or strain to reach notes that seem unattainable, if your voice were 100 percent relaxed, you couldn't sing at all. Your vocal muscles have to contract when you sing, because muscles contract. That's how they work. It's a matter of degree.

On the other hand, many singers believe (incorrectly) that pushing the voice hard is the *only* way to get that raw, exciting, edgy sound that is prevalent in many musical styles, and also loud enough to be heard over a band! They may believe it is the only way they can achieve that "raspy" sound that is so desirable in many contemporary styles. This is not true, and can be harmful.

TIP: Avoid Excessive Force When You Sing

Singing with a lot of additional force brings the vocal folds together with increased velocity. This means your voice is getting hammered and abraded. (Please see the section called "Get More Sound with Less Work" later in this chapter.) This approach is definitely not advisable and may result in vocal fatigue, even hoarseness. Whenever your voice feels tired, hoarse, or sore after you sing, your body is warning you to stop. You probably overdid it.

You may be concerned instead that by pushing your voice, you will simply *sound bad*. (You may be equating the idea of pushing with using your chest voice, especially if that lower register is a part of the voice that you don't use often or at all.) I used to believe this. As a soprano, when I first started exploring my lower full voice, I thought it was *hideous* sounding. Truly horrid! I would sing a note then stop it as soon as it emerged, without giving it a chance. I continued exploring this voice only because a good friend of mine, who is a skilled pop/rock guitar player, encouraged me to continue. "The sound isn't ugly," he would say. "It's strong. It's not *pretty*, but so what? It's interesting, it has character." Once I stopped worrying about having a "pretty" voice all the time, as I had been taught, I was much less tense and could explore this voice freely. I found power in this range. Expression. A new rock and blues voice. It was incredibly exciting.

Myth Two: Belting Requires Super Physical Bodily Strength

You may believe that besides pushing out your voice, you need to exert extreme physical effort throughout your body in order to achieve a belt sound, such as exhausting diaphragmatic breathing or XTreme workouts on stage. This is not true. Remember, you want to last. You want a voice that sounds great after a three-hour gig, that can gig several nights a week, *and* that has years of singing ahead of you. You don't want to poop out!

Sometimes, we put on a dramatic show of strength and power for our audiences. No problem there. Acting is part of what makes a performer charismatic, and can give a performance the appearance of exerting more effort than what the singer really needed to sing well. This is one important way that singers endure over many years of performing. One of my favorite stories conveys this point very well, which I relate in my book *Your Singing Voice: Contemporary Techniques, Expression and Spirit*" (pages 185–6). This story, told to me by the celebrated and veteran vocalist Patti Austin, describes how a little acting changed her audience's perception of what she was singing. As the story goes, after a long day of recording advertising jingles, she and the other professional singers in her group recorded a perfect take. But the client felt the recording was lackluster and asked them to do it again. Although the singers knew the take sounded great, they went along with the client's wishes. They put smiles on their faces and added some energetic, enthusiastic movements as they rerecorded it. The client was quite pleased with the result, saying, "You've got it! That's it!" I asked Patti, "Didn't the additional movement and energy make your singing better?" "No," she replied. How did she know? After the client left, the group listened back to the two recordings side by side. They were identical in every way! Their acting had given the client the physical energy he was missing while watching them sing, but it had made no difference in the final recording. The singers were *that good* at separating their audience's *perception* of their heightened physical energy from what was actually happening internally as they sang. They used the appropriate amount of energy to sing as always, but to get this great sound, it was not necessary to put on a big show. The extra acting did, however, help their client to get more excited about what he heard.

This story illustrates the point that pushing yourself physically all the time, exerting maximum effort every time you sing by giving 110 percent, is not necessary. It only wears you out! Even machines wear out, and you are not a machine. I always recommend instead giving 80 percent physically, while still staying 100 percent focused in the present moment. Save the rest of your energy to recharge yourself, to give back to you. How can you give your best performance if you're exhausted? It is up to you to know your physical limits and respect them. No one else will do this for you.

You can learn your limits by comparing singing to your other physical activities. If you do a long-distance run or another type of extended cardiac exercise, you need to pace yourself. Many begin to experience a flow, an evenness to your pacing once past the first ten to fifteen minutes of exertion. Your breathing stabilizes. You may even "relax into" the exercise, even though your body is working hard. Endorphins may be released and you begin to enjoy the exercise. On the other hand, if you run your body too hard while you exert yourself, saying to yourself, "faster, faster, faster!" you are introducing stress. Although this may be useful for an Olympic race, you can only maintain that pace for so long before tiring. As singers, we expect ourselves to sing routinely for hours at a stretch and for years to come. (Producers and others who do not sing often demand this of us, too.) But if you think about it, can you expect your voice—which is a tiny, sensitive area of muscle and tissue—to be stronger than your *legs*? More durable than a highly trained, highly disciplined Olympian athlete?

Myth Three: Belting Uses Only Chest Voice

This is perhaps the most common and potentially harmful myth about belt singing. If there is only one concept that you take away from reading this book, this is it!

Many people believe that when you belt, you always drive your lower voice (*chest voice*) up as high as it can go. This is perhaps why so many people are afraid of belting. They know that singing high and loud in chest voice is constrained by their voice's size and shape, and while they may feel this constraint when they sing, they still want that sound that belting offers. What a conflict to navigate!

> *"You do not have to (and should not) rely exclusively on your chest voice to belt."*

This limitation often leads people to tend to push their voices too hard to compensate, which is very fatiguing—even vocally damaging—especially if overused or abused. The ill effects of forcing the voice beyond its limits usually show up afterwards in a fatigued or hoarse speaking voice.

Belting is a kind of loud singing that ascends to medium-high notes for women and to high notes for men, depending on vocal type. For women, the height of a belt range is typically the notes F4 (F above middle C) to E5; for men, it is C4 (middle C) to B5. As we saw in chapter 2, what we call *chest voice* occurs when the vocal folds press together firmly to create a thickened area of contact, using increased air pressure from your lungs to create a stronger sound. Meanwhile, as you raise the pitch, the vocal folds stretch longer. Therefore, if you use only chest voice to belt, as you ascend to these high notes, your voice pulls aggressively in two opposing directions, resisting the need to thin for the higher pitch. If you continue this past the point of anatomical comfort, vocal strain will definitely result. Instead, when you belt in a healthy, sustainable way, you rely mostly on *mix voice* for the highest pitches, switching to chest voice for lower notes. Sometimes, too, you can use mix voice throughout a passage. It all depends upon the song and style you are singing, the song's range, and the dynamics. In the section beginning on page 42, "Mix Voice: The Secret Recipe for Success," I discuss how to access this voice and use it consistently. Also take a look later in this chapter at the section called "Women: Yes, Use Your Chest Voice and Embrace Your Mix."

> *"When you belt in a healthy, sustainable way, you rely mostly on **mix voice** for the highest pitches, switching to chest voice for lower notes."*

SHIFTING YOUR APPROACH

These myths about belting get in the way of success. So, let's shift your approach. There's an old adage that goes something like, "If you continue traveling on the road you're on, in the direction you are facing, you'll end up where you are headed." So, how do you change course and still belt successfully, wisely, and healthfully? The answer: get off the road, and shift your focus.

> *"Instead of asking, 'How do I belt?' ask, 'How can I sing with more volume?'"*

The first step toward this goal is to reframe the way you state it. Instead of asking, "How do I belt?" ask, "How can I sing with more volume?"

PREPARING FOR SUCCESSFUL BELTING

Now that we've left the old myths behind, let's look at how you can belt healthfully with volume and a bright, engaging sound.

First, remember that when you belt, your goal is to be loud. Singing with more volume. What makes something loud? *High frequencies* in the sound contribute significantly to volume. High-pitched tones travel farther and appear louder than lower-pitched tones. What are some loud (even piercing) sounds you can think of? An alarm clock. Babies wailing. A car horn. A pistol firing. A soprano singing high C.

Understanding Volume and Singing Louder

To sing louder, you want to add higher frequencies to your tone. What does this mean? Volume is measured in *decibels*,[5] abbreviated "dB." A tone's *frequency* (highs or lows) is measured in Hertz, abbreviated "Hz." Again for reference, using our present-day tuning system, the note middle C (C4) is 261.63 Hz, and A4 just above that is 440 Hz. Compare these notes to an alarm clock's stirring ring that sits at 8,000 Hz (well above the top note on a piano) and wakes you with 80 dB of volume. A car horn honking from 15 feet away is loudest around the note C7, 2,093 Hz. Songbirds, with tiny bodies and voices that carry quite a distance, don't even enter the frequency spectrum below 2,000 Hz. A baby's cry gets mom's attention also around 2,000 Hz and at a formidable 120 dB, whereas this author's soprano high C6 at 1,046.50 Hz—two octaves up from middle C and a fourth below the top of my range—has been clocked at 115 to 120 Hz! (Singing that loudly even hurts my ears.) Figure 3.2 gives you a sampling of different sound sources, their frequencies measured in Hz, and how loud that sounds when measured in decibels.

Sound Source	125 Hz C3 = 130.81 Hz	250 Hz C4 = 261.63 Hz	500 Hz C5 = 523.25 Hz	1,000 Hz C6 = 1,046.5 Hz	2,000 Hz C7=2,093 Hz	4,000 Hz C8 = 4,186 Hz	8,000 Hz
Normal Conversation at 3'	—	91 dB	91 dB	87 dB	83 dB	79 dB	66 dB
Birds	—	—	—	—	50 dB	52 dB	54 dB
Alarm Clock at 4–9'	—	—	—	—	—	70 dB	80 dB
Baby's Cry	—	—	—	—	120 dB	—	—
Pistol Shot at 250'	—	—	83 dB	91 dB	99 dB	102 dB	106 dB
Car Horn at 15'	—	—	92 dB	95 dB	990 dB	80 dB	60 dB
Author Singing C6 Loudly	—	—	—	115 dB	—	—	—

FIG. 3.2. Noise Levels. Adapted from www.acousticalsolutions.com/noise-level-chart.

---

5. Decibel measurements are exponential, not linear. Every 10 dB increase is a doubling in perceived volume.

Looking at the decibel chart you can see that volume does not necessarily correlate to size. For example, as loud as a pistol shot may be when fired from 250 feet away, it is still softer than my own high C when measured from about 10 feet. The loudest instruments are not always the biggest. A piercing ref's whistle is very small, and so is a commanding baby's voice.

Why is this discussion relevant to belting? Your voice is small. The length of the average woman's vocal folds is only 1.5 cm (a little over half an inch), and a man's only slightly longer at 2 cm (about three quarters of an inch). So how can this tiny structure possibly create all the sound we produce in singing and speaking?

Air. Air is (mostly) the whole enchilada. You don't have to force muscles to overwork in order to be heard. Your air does it for you. The secret to reduced-stress singing: release excess tension. Focus closely, listen to your sound and pitch, then stop controlling everything. Trust your air. Feed your body full and calm inhalations down into your core as needed. Then, release the air calmly, but with balanced strength. Your voice will respond.

Breath Management

We spend a lot of time discussing breathing in voice lessons, since managing your air is such an integral part of singing in a successful and healthy way. As we've seen, singing uses a combination of many physical and mental actions that occur simultaneously. In chapter 2, we looked at how your breathing system works, specifically the interaction of your diaphragm, intercostal, and abdominal muscles with the parts in your larynx. Good singing technique in any style enables maintaining air pressure in the body longer than is needed to speak, but without adding unnecessary tension, such as lifting your shoulders or over-tightening your stomach.

Perhaps because anyone who talks about "proper" singing technique will usually warn you about breathing correctly, too often singers actually *over-*breathe. This is especially true with belting. Many stuff themselves with gulps of air with the belief that maximum inhalation is always the best approach. Not true! Don't confuse *managing* your air as you sing with sucking in huge quantities of air every time you inhale before a phrase. It's the *management of the air you have* that is the most important aspect of effective belting.

You're not drowning, just singing! Breathing for singing is a matter of degree and coordination. True, if you use too little air (inadequate support), you may tend to over-squeeze your throat (pharynx constrictor muscles) to achieve the sound you want, especially when you belt, causing your voice to strain and tire. Or, you may take in a good breath but loose it quickly through a breathy tone. But if you use *too much* air, you will not only tire more quickly; you also add unnecessary tension to your thoracic and laryngeal muscles and will likely strain your voice. Your lungs *always* have air in them, unless you have a collapsed lung, which is a very serious medical condition. In fact, one can actually *exhale* and still sing with the air remaining in your lungs, which I have shown in Demonstration Video 29. (Please don't try this unless you are an advanced singer. This "parlor trick" is provided to illustrate the point, but it is definitely not a suggested vocal approach.)

29

As you improve your singing technique, you learn to release air in a directed way in order to support the sound you're going for. The air flow works together with the vocal folds themselves to create a kind of resistance. The air you exhale as you sing, coming from the *glottis* space beneath the area of your vocal folds, must be sufficiently pressurized in order to produce sound. This is referred to as *sub-glottal pressure*. You learn to adjust how much air you really need, in direct collaboration with how your vocal folds respond, depending on what you are singing. When you belt, the vocal edges press together more firmly as the air pressure increases.

Supported breathing can feel somewhat like simply holding your breath, while releasing air slowly and steadily. Try this exercise to experience the sensation. Then, practice the breathing exercises provided at the beginning of part II.

Exercise: Long Steady Breath Release ("SSS" or Hiss)

1

This breath exercise is designed to show you how air pressure can be controlled. You coordinate your abdominal muscles with a small resistance in your mouth that reduces the airflow. It uses the same principle as holding one long note.

1. Draw in a slow, comfortable, and deep breath, taking care not to over-stuff yourself with air. Hold your breath for a count of 2.

2. Begin to release the air on a hissing sound ("sss") while creating resistance with your tongue and teeth, and contracting your upper abs slightly. Hiss fairly loudly for a count of 12, as if you were a valve releasing gas. Listen to the sound, keeping it steady.

3. Let's see how long you can make the hissing sound last on this one breath. Count to 12 as you exhale on the hiss. Now, breathe in again slowly, hold your breath for 2 counts, and repeat the hiss to a count of 16.

4. On your next breath, count to 20 while you hiss. Repeat.

5. Now try it once again, this time hissing even longer. Can you make it past a count of 20 without feeling like you are straining? Try it again. What can you adjust to make the sound last longer? A helpful approach is to use less air at the beginning and then to apply more pressure from your abdomen towards the end as your air volume decreases.

6. Repeat the exercise two more times, while attempting to make the hiss last even longer. There's no magic number; if you can't make it to 20 at first, that is okay. You'll become more coordinated and find you can do this for longer phrases, the more you practice.

7. Don't push your breath so hard that you become light-headed! It should feel easy, relaxing. In fact, this exercise might even put in you a calm state.

> *"The beginning of the phrase is when you want to **resist** releasing the air, as you concentrate on producing the steady hissing sound. Then, as your air begins to run low while you continue hissing, you will have more air left in order to keep the sound at a steady volume."*

Pay attention to what part of your body needs to be in charge for the hiss to be easy yet stable. Are your shoulders relaxed? Are you over-squeezing and tensing your mouth? Remember, at the beginning of the phrase there is more pressure in your lungs. This makes producing the sound easier at first. The beginning of the phrase is when you want to *resist* releasing the air, as you concentrate on producing the steady hissing sound. Then, as your air begins to run low while you continue hissing, you will have more air left in order to keep the sound at a steady volume.

Keep in mind: when you sing, it is a focused physical activity, such as easy-going swimming, balancing as you glide downhill on a pair of skis, or taking a brisk walk. The difference is that when you sing, you do not need to feed large leg muscles additional oxygen. The similarity is that while singing is active and focused, you can still be at ease.

TIP: Prepare Your Breath

Whenever you can, TAKE TIME to prepare your breath. If you have a measure of rest in a song, for example, use that moment to breathe in slowly and prepare the next phrase mentally. This even works if you have just a beat or two to breathe in. It is important *not* to wait until the last second to suck in a breath. That only throws your vocal mechanism off balance, and it will make your pitch shakier, too. Slow breathing also keeps you calmer—a nice plus.

Belting takes more air pressure than singing at a neutral volume. When you belt notes lower in your range, you need to increase the amount of air that meets your vocal folds, to help bring them together more firmly. This increased air supports the work of the TA muscles, as they thicken your vocal folds where they meet in vibration.

Belting with Less Impact

Remember this important rule: Anytime you sing with more volume, the force that brings your vocal folds together in contact is stronger. This means the edges of the folds themselves hit together with increased impact or velocity, making them more likely to be affected than when you use less force. It is a logical, cause-effect result.

Pressure in your voice itself is not as concerning as the way you bring your voice together in vibration. You need pressure to sing, but forcing your voice to get the sound you want—which too many belters do all the time—is risky. It is important to learn to begin a phrase without squeezing your throat too hard. This is force. A forced start to a note is sometimes called a *glottal attack*.

"Glottal Attack"

A *glottal attack* is a kind of forced impact that sounds like a burst of air escaping from your voice, almost like a hard grunt. Although it is a sound so common in popular singing these days that you may not even notice you're doing it, singing with frequent glottal attacks is one of the leading causes of vocal fatigue. It happens when the voice is held closed too tightly before you begin a note. Then, the force of air pressure from your lungs causes your vocal folds to burst apart as the puffs-of-air cycle begins, and they slam shut once again. (See "Larynx: Your Tone Generator" in chapter 2 to review how the folds rely on puffs of air to function.) The glottal attack can also happen in the opposite way, when your glottis (the space in between your vocal folds) begins in an open position but is forced shut as you begin to sing. This action happens so fast that you may not even notice it without the keen ear of a knowledgeable teacher.

> *"Learn to begin a phrase without squeezing your throat too hard, and without starting each phrase with force."*

To experience a glottal attack, try this: First say, "ugh ugh ugh!" Now say, "ha ha ha." The sound "ugh" contains a glottal attack: in order to make this sound, your throat closes somewhat while you phonate. In contrast, when you say "ha," your vocal folds part enough to let out the air contained in an "h" sound. That parting inhibits a glottal attack. Sometimes, a voice teacher will have you say "ha" to learn to be aware of a glottal-attack tendency. On the other hand, you may be a singer who "leaks air," as if you're a tire or balloon with a pinhole in it. If this is you, you will run out of air rapidly when you sing. This happens when your vocal folds don't quite meet, letting air escape too rapidly while you sing. You can probably recognize which tendency is yours: glottal attack, or a breathy sound that loses air quickly.

TIP: Belting Habits That Hinder Your Singing

Ironically, many belters have both frustrating habits! They use glottal attacks when they belt, but they also leak air on softer tones. This is usually because the laryngeal muscles are accustomed to an all-or-nothing approach. "ARE YOU IN OR ARE YOU OUT?" To work on smoothing out these habits, develop your medium-volume notes without belting. Also work on sustaining clean, soft tones. Both of these approaches are practiced in part II (see "Exercise 5. Clean "Neutral" Tones, Using Chromatics" and "Exercise 7. Developing Mix Voice").

High Pitch = Increased Impact

Another reason the vocal folds can come together with high impact is the pitch. High notes increase impact on the voice. As we have seen, when you ascend in pitch, the rate of speed at which your folds vibrate against one another increases. The combination of velocity from volume, and rate of contact from the note, intensifies the potential pounding of the vocal edges together, increasing your risk for vocal fatigue, swelling, even injury. This is why women's voices are generally more prone to injury than men's: singing high frequencies, a woman's vocal folds come together in vibration many more times per second than the notes in most male ranges. The exception to this is when a man sings high tenor notes that are the same frequencies as notes in a woman's range; in those cases, the same velocity is at work.

Each Voice Is Unique

Generally speaking, most instruments such as guitar, piano, bass, and so on will be similar to one another in how they function, even though their body styles, tones, and touch are not identical. For example, it is reasonable to expect that all tenor saxophones share a common array of valves and fingering, even though there is a wide range of metals, mouthpieces, and reeds through which the sax is played. The human voice, however, is a very different story.

We come in all shapes and sizes, and so do our voices. Besides our varying vocal types, each person's voice holds up differently. We use our voices differently, too. Some people can sing for hours at a time with no ill effects, while others cannot. Some singers belt throughout their lifetimes and keep on going, yet others cannot belt for more than a couple of songs without fatigue. Genetics play a significant role in endurance, and other factors such as daily self-care, sleep, diet, illness, and stress also play a large role, varying widely from person to person.

If you hope to sound like your favorite singing artist, you may be disappointed. You are you. You sound like you. Your endurance is different from other people's. Your bone structure, muscle structure, height, weight, strength, flexibility, tolerance, and sensitivity are all part of what make you unique. The shapes and durability of your vocal structures, and your ear's receptiveness to pitch and tone, also contribute to your unique sound. Your beliefs about what sounds good or bad play a significant role in how you sing. So do your aesthetic preferences. How is an iconic performer like Bruce Springsteen still singing and playing hard through super-long concerts, singing with a gravelly voice, even after decades of doing it? (When you watch him sing, he seems to be working very hard!) It's because his anatomy—his constitution—makes it possible. Why did the great Whitney Houston's voice tragically lose its luster and quality relatively early? It was due to a combination of her anatomy, how she used her voice in concert, her response to stress, and her self-care. The artist you emulate may not even be achieving the sound you're after in the same exact way you are attempting it. Everyone gets results a little differently. Often, too—especially recently—tricks in the recording studio create superhuman vocals out of mere mortals. Don't be fooled by what you hear in other singers.[6] What does this mean? We each sing differently, even when we sound similar. Each person sings with his or her own complex blend of physical movements and thought, much of which is unconscious. What is important is what works, *for you.*

As you progress through learning demanding vocal styles such as belting, proceed cautiously until you have learned your own strengths and weaknesses. Listen to your body. If your voice gets tired—or worse, hoarse—stop for now.

The Zen of Belting: Mindfulness

All singing requires a solid foundation of support from your whole self, both in body and in awareness. Belting, because it is a very demanding (even athletic) way to sing, requires you to pay close attention to what you're doing. Be mindful when you belt. Keep observing how your voice responds. As you prepare to sing, observe your breath. When you take in a breath before a phrase, notice: are you bracing yourself, expecting an outcome? Do you inhale at the last second, like a gasp or a gulp? Or, do you take time to inhale calmly, slower? Next, observe how your voice feels and responds while you sing, and how it feels after you've sung. Just as an athlete has an inner barometer monitoring his or her progress, you must learn to stay mentally "in the game" whenever you sing with force. Your body language may not reveal this effort outwardly to an audience, but inwardly, to sing at your best, you are continually aware and focused.

---

6. In a recent voice study, each subject in a group of professional singers was monitored with advanced vocal apparatus while singing identical-sounding tones and volumes. What could not be observed visually by watching their singing, even by the medical laryngologist experts conducting the tests, was measured by the equipment. The result: no two singers, though their sounds matched seamlessly, created the tones in the same way.

Mindfulness, ideally self-awareness with patient detachment, gives you the opportunity to monitor yourself as you sing. Is your voice hoarse or tired when you stop? That is a sign you have overdone it or stepped out of balance. You may be singing out of frustration; or, perhaps the artist you emulate seems to be able to sing well past your own limit; or, perhaps your friend seems to sing loudly and strongly without rustling a feather. Remember, when we are frustrated we become tense, even annoyed. Attempting anything as physically coordinated as singing from a place of too much tension will only make it harder. And more frustrating. And harder. And even more frustrating. And then you may say to yourself, "WHY CAN'T I DO THIS?" Yes, you are correct, you can't. Because you just planned and practiced failure. How do you get a more satisfactory result? Change the process. Shift your strategy. Try something different.

> *"How do you get a different result? Change the process. Shift your strategy. Try something different."*

Practicing from a place of mindfulness—from patience, and self-forgiveness, especially if you don't reach your goal at first as you'd hoped—*allows* you to meet your goal. Ironic, isn't it?

The truth is, whenever you fight yourself, one of you will lose. So, don't fight. Embrace. And most of all, be patient.

MIX VOICE: THE SECRET RECIPE FOR SUCCESS

So, if belting isn't all chest voice, as we discussed earlier in the section "Myth Three" (page 33), how can you belt safely? Using *mix voice* is the secret ingredient. Mix voice allows you to belt higher notes without straining. Mix voice means just what it sounds like: a little bit of this, a little bit of that. There is no exact recipe.

As we saw in chapter 2, your voice has two basic vocal registers that work together most of the time when you sing or speak. Your lower register is TA-dominant, pressing your vocal edges together and shortening them. Your higher register is CT-dominant, created by the rocking forward of the thyroid cartilage that stretches the vocal folds longer as pitch rises; this motion also causes the vocal folds to thin. Most of where you use your voice is somewhere in the middle of this spectrum, utilizing both muscle groups together. As we also saw in chapter 2, these two muscle groups usually move in opposing directions simultaneously. This is normal. Most singing, especially by women, routinely uses a blend of TA and CT muscles. That is mix voice.

By allowing your voice to stretch and thin as you ascend in pitch, even as you keep air pressure strong and frequencies in your mouth bright for louder notes, you can learn to achieve a formidable belt sound using mix voice.

For both men and women, using a mix voice for belting high, loud notes provides volume and bright timbre with the least amount of wear and tear on the voice. Sometimes, narrowing your pharynx (the back of your throat) a bit will help to create a brighter, louder sound. This is a normal function of singing. How? Put the sound into the roof of your mouth, or make it sound thinner. Although pressing more of your vocal folds together while you push air against them will give you more volume, so will increasing the overtones in your sound. To explore your overtones, see exercise 8 in part II.

There is a broad spectrum of tones in the mix voice that includes a big part of your range. The quality of a mix voice note comes down to how you *place* it in your mouth, specifically how you shape the vowel. Belting is bright. It is forward. Avoid keeping the sound too far back in your throat or too "dark." Mix placement can produce higher frequencies and volume because of how you shape your mouth and tongue. Watch Video Demonstration 7 to see some ways of using mix voice.

7

Try this next exercise in order to experience singing a vibrant sound. It is a technique to enable you to find bright placement. You can blend this sound into your overall singing later, but for now, let's discover the sound in a pure form.

Exercise: Bright "Ee" Vowel

Sing an "Ee" vowel to imitate a twangy sound such as the Wicked Witch of the West, or Elmo from *Sesame Street*. Sing this sound at a moderate volume as you imitate the character, on a simple five-note descent from B♭. The sound will be very bright. (You may find it unappealing, but give it a shot anyway.) Be mindful that you don't overdo it by squeezing your throat too tightly. For women, these notes may pass through a transition area. Stick with the tone anyway. For most men these notes, when sung down an octave, will be in a comfortable part of your range. High tenors can try them as written, beginning above middle C.

Ee _____

FIG. 3.3. Bright "Ee" Vowel Exercise

Was the sound during this exercise louder than normal? You may feel silly imitating a witch or a puppet. Silly is okay! Don't worry, you are not singing in this way permanently. (If you don't experiment, how can you expect to find new ways of singing?) Improving your singing technique means looking for a *strategy* to find the sound you're after. Just be sure you are not over-constricting the back of your throat to make this sound. The tongue should be relaxed, but peaked enough in your mouth to create a real "Ee." Now, try repeating the exercise while moving your tongue around. Observe how the sound and effort change. When you hit on the spot that has the most sound with the least feeling of effort, that's your golden nugget.

> *"Improving your singing technique means looking for a **strategy** to find the sound you're after."*

The exercises provided in part II take you through more strategies for finding a bright sound suitable for belting with your own vocal instrument.

SINGING *THROUGH* THE "BREAK"

Your full vocal range is a system with flexible, moveable parts. Understanding it in this way, rather than as a box with fixed settings, switches, and levers, gives you more agility to move through your registers with ease and accuracy. It's a form of letting go, while working on coordination for fine motor control.

When you allow your voice to lighten slightly with each note as you ascend in pitch, the CT muscles continue to stretch while the TAs gradually let go. It's a push-me-pull-you system. This is how you avoid an obvious "break"—singing *through* it instead. Yes, your voice is transitioning, parts are moving, but they don't have to move jerkily. However, if you *don't* thin out the sound as you ascend, your anatomy reaches its limit and you cannot bring this forced sound any higher. You have reached a boundary, your voice shifts suddenly into head voice to release the pressure, and the quality of your voice shifts dramatically and quickly. This is a common problem belters experience. Knowing this is coming, most people suck back the sound or skip over that spot, avoiding it. They become anxious to learn from a teacher where their "break" is so they can steer clear of it. When using only chest voice to belt, many people try to push past their natural limit, squeezing, craning, scrunching. Wearing out. This is definitely *not* a good idea!

We are now at the point at which reading about vocal technique becomes tricky. You have to discover how to sing with your own body, through changes in your larynx, and with your own unique voice. The video examples provided online are designed to show you the different sounds described here, and to give you exercises to practice. The online demonstrations by myself and with four young singers—two women and two men—are provided so you can observe different belt voices. Please refer to Demonstration Video 26, "Your 'Break' and Blending Registers" to watch a vivid demonstration of what the break is and how to sing in and out of belt voice more smoothly. Record yourself as you practice so you can hear and observe any changes. And remember, these exercises should feel like you are free of excess tension.

26

GET MORE SOUND WITH LESS WORK

When we form words for singing high notes, the vowels need to be rounder and broader than they are in everyday speech. You can still sing true vowels—except on the highest, loudest notes—but they are more open. This not only increases the resonant space in your mouth, it also helps to relieve some of the pull on your voice. This gets you more sound with less work.

One tried-and-true method to keep your vowels open is to wait until the very end of a word before you complete it or close it off with the ending consonant. Sing the open part of the vowel, instead. For example:

The vowel "I" is actually a complex sound. It is a triphthong with three tones: "ah" + "ay" + "ee."

Ah _____ ay _____ ee

FIG. 3.4. The Triphthongs in the Spoken Vowel "I"

When you sing loudly and high on the sound "I," hold the "Ah" sound until the very end of the note, then breeze through ay-ee at the end. In this way you are singing the most open sound in the word, rather than the tight "ee" at the end of the triphthong.

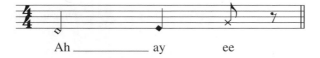

Ah _____ ay   ee

FIG. 3.5. Lengthen "Ah" when Singing an "I" Vowel

Sing the word "my." It has the same vowel sound as "I," preceded by an "m" consonant. To belt this word, get off the "m" quickly and right to the "Ah" sound as in "I," and again complete the ay-ee at the tail end of the note.

The part of a word that is the easiest to belt is its vowel. Try this out: sing the word "bring." This word is sung and belted many times in "Bring Him Home" from *Les Misérables*, for example. "Bring" can be broken down into five sounds: "ba," "rr," "ih," "ee" and "ng." If you sing it without breaking down the word, your voice will get tight, as in "briNG!" This happens because "ng," which ends the word, is a closed sound in your throat. Instead, get to the the "ih" sound quickly: "b-rr-IH-ee…ng," spending most of your time on the "ih" sound. Or, if "ee" is a better sound for you, land on that vowel instead. Then, when you move to the next note in the melody, connect "ng" to it. This will make "bring" understandable even though you were holding out the vowel "ih."

Your Tongue Muscle and Pharynx

Your tongue is an extremely strong muscle capable of complex multitasking movements. It can articulate language clearly and still be contracted in the back; you can sing a vowel that sounds right, even though your tongue is pulling back simultaneously and tightening your voice. Especially when you belt, which can add more stress to your voice muscles, your tongue should be as relaxed as possible, *especially* in the back.

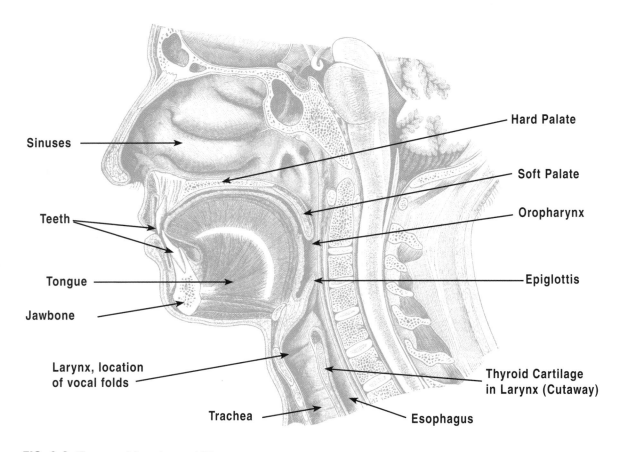

FIG. 3.6. Tongue Muscle and Pharynx

Your tongue shapes vowels and helps you to swallow. It is a highly complex, sophisticated muscle that sits deep in your mouth and jaw. Connected to the top of your vocal process via the *hyoid bone*, the tongue affects how your voice responds. Sometimes when a singer's voice fatigues easily or does not respond well, the hidden culprit is an overly tight tongue. Here are three exercises to manage tongue tension.

1. Stick your tongue out and release. Repeat ten times.

2. Massage the base of your tongue from under your chin, on either side of your larynx, under your throat. Be mindful not to press too hard.

3. Hold the tip of your tongue while you sing an open vowel like "ah" or "ee."

FIG. 3.7. Tongue Tension Release Exercise. A major scale on open vowels, for practicing singing without tongue tension.

TIP: Tongue Release

To practice releasing your tongue, sing while you hold the tip of it. (Wash your hands first. If it's too gross to hold your tongue with your fingers, use a gauze pad or paper towel instead.) Does your tongue retract, seeming to want to pull backwards? If yes, this tells you you've been singing with an overly tight tongue. To help your tongue loosen its grip, regularly practice singing while holding it. Yes, holding your tongue definitely makes articulating words more difficult! Try singing just the vowels of the lyric as you hold your tongue. The benefit of this practice is teaching you how to form words with less tension in your throat.

In the *pharynx*—the back of your throat—you have important constrictor muscles. They are designed to protect your voice, to help you swallow, and to keep your airway clear. They also contribute to the tone of your voice. Sometimes, we squeeze the throat a little bit to achieve a brighter tone. This is normal. Again, it is a matter of degree. When you go for a sound but are also mindful of adequate air support and staying as relaxed as possible overall, you are less likely to strain or tire your voice. On the other hand, if you think you need to tense up in order to get the sound you want, your body will comply. If you over-constrict your pharynx, it makes singing much more difficult.

MEN: APPROACHING THE PASSAGGIO

Belting is a bit different for men than for women, because most men sing primarily in full voice, whereas women jump routinely in between full voice and lighter approaches. In many popular songs, singing a melody to the height of the full voice is business as usual for men. However, to keep ascending past that range, men reach a point where they either *have* to shift gears into a lighter sound—such as mix voice or falsetto—or they've reached their melodic limit. The passaggio, a thinner area of transition between registers, is where men navigate into falsetto while shifting muscle dominance.

Male belting can also mean loud singing above the passaggio, by using a strong and "buzzing" mix voice instead of full voice. Though men use mix voice less often, it can be the best, most effective way to belt out loud, high notes. Two examples of male rock singers who do this are Lou Gramm of Foreigner, and Freddie Mercury of Queen. This mix is a blend between falsetto and full voice where some of the actual vocal folds are in vibration but they've become very thin. Some men find this placement naturally; others have to learn to find it.

Everyone wants to skip over the icky bits and sound great right away. That won't help you to improve. The best way to practice your passaggio transition area is to embrace it, as if looking at it under a magnifying glass. "Isn't that jerky area interesting!" you can tell yourself. By singing *through* the passaggio, not *around* it, you will develop better control in that area. You want to nurture the areas of your voice you don't like and work through them, patiently. Patience is the key. Especially if you don't like how you sound now. You may be amazed later at what you can sing! But first, you have to give your voice a chance.

WOMEN: YES, USE YOUR CHEST VOICE, AND EMBRACE YOUR MIX

Should women avoid singing in chest voice? The answer for popular styles is a profound "no!" in spite of commonly held beliefs in some training methods that declare a woman's chest voice is too strenuous or sounds unappealing. If the music sits low in a woman's range where she doesn't have much volume, she can learn to use her chest voice safely to make the sound fuller. Because a woman's larynx is usually smaller than a man's, the average woman's lower range does not descend as far. Most young women don't sing much below G3 (below middle C). Middle C, C4, is usually comfortable but on the low side for many young women, yet getting toward the high side for men. To achieve a strong belt sound, women will often bring their full (chest) voice up toward F4, G4, even A4 and above. Most women's voices will want to transition into a lighter tone around E4 to F4.

This is why belting can be so difficult: many popular melodies sit in awkward areas of the average woman's vocal anatomy. (This has changed over the years. Listen back to popular songs from decades ago, and you'll hear women singing where their voices sound natural and unforced. Popular melody ranges for women have definitely lowered in recent years.) However, as long as the melody does not go *too* high, most women can sing it comfortably in chest voice. But just like the guys, this also poses a limit. A melodic ceiling. A hard "break" point. Singing continually only in chest voice also makes softer tones more challenging to access, because the vocal muscles become accustomed to working in only one way.

To develop a belt sound that is flexible instead and less forced-sounding with more melodic options, practice non-belted tones that are sung softly, and cleanly! This may seem counterintuitive. Remember, singing technique is about developing fine motor control and coordination. By singing soft, clean tones, your voice can learn to gain finer dexterity. Mix voice in particular helps to belt out high notes, especially when you sing with a bright "forward" tone that glides between notes without giant shifts or "breaks." This will help you to develop a vocal tonal palette that has many options, instead of brick-wall limits. And with a mix voice's overtones blended into the sound, you can train your belt voice to be even stronger and more effective than 100 percent chest-voice belting. Remember, it's not an either/or recipe. Watch Demonstration Video 30, "Have Some Fun: Different Ways to Belt," to see how you can blend mix voice, head voice, and chest voice all on one riffed phrase.

SELECTING YOUR KEY

The range of notes in the average popular song usually stays within an octave or so. When you belt, it's important that you find the key that works best for *your* voice. If you need to transpose a song to a different key to suit your voice, that shift is often no more than an interval of a fourth (either up or down), and frequently even less.

Stylistically, today's popular songs often sit high in a man's range and lower in a woman's. Many popular male singers are tenors or high baritones. Many popular female singers are altos or second sopranos. Yet the average male voice is a baritone, while the average (especially younger) female voice is a soprano. Keep this in mind when you compare your voice to the original singer.

Sometimes, even a transposition of only a half step can make a big difference in how your voice responds to the melody.

Follow these basic tips to select a key.

1. Unless you are performing with a fixed score, there is absolutely no need to stay in the original key. It is not a badge of honor to be able to sing in the same key as Freddie Mercury or Aretha Franklin or Ariana Grande. The key needs to work for your voice, *your* sound. We've already heard the original artist. We want to hear *you* now.

2. Where is the hook or "payoff" of the song? In popular styles, that is often the chorus. Where does the melody sit in your voice? If the melody lingers at a transition point where you are on the cusp of your lighter (head) voice, try lowering or raising the key. The last thing you want to do is strain when you sing this part of the tune.

3. What are the lowest notes? The highest? Make sure the entire melody fits comfortably within your range. If the notes are low on the bottom but still reachable, the microphone may be sufficient to amplify them, so you can sing the higher, demanding part of the tune without straining.

4. Listen to the overall quality of how your voice sounds on the song. It may sound quite different when you change keys.

5. Consider the age of the song relative to today's aesthetics. Early popular songs, for example, many of which became belting standards later, were originally written to be sung fairly high. Many singers will lower the keys today to alter the quality of the melodies in the voice. Two examples of these standards are "Ain't Misbehavin'" (1929, Razaf/Waller/Brooks), written in the key of E♭, and "People Will Say We're in Love" (from *Oklahoma!*, 1943, Rogers/Hammerstein) written in the key of C. Although these songs might be belted today, they were both written for soprano/tenor, years before belting became so popular.

6. Is the original song for a man or for a woman? Consider this when you select the key. A common transposition for a woman singing a man's song is an interval of a fourth down, and up a forth for a man singing a woman's tune.

7. Finally, consider the key signature. If the key could be either F or F♯, choose F. Keys with four or fewer sharps or flats will be smoother for your accompanist(s) or band mates to play.

MICROPHONE TECHNIQUE

In popular styles, the microphone becomes an extension of your voice. It allows you to sing at any volume and to be heard above a band. Learn to utilize a mic to its fullest advantage. When you sing softly, you can be close to the mic, about the distance equal to the width of your hand. If you are singing at a whisper volume, you can get very close (but be careful of popping out consonants). When you sing loudly, you need to add a couple of inches or so between your mouth and the mic so it does not feed back or distort. Practice with a mic often to get the hang of it.

A mic will also change how you hear yourself. You don't want to be surprised on the gig. PA systems vary, and mics vary. These affect how you sound. The room acoustics also affect your sound, which can bounce around (such as in a hall with reflective surfaces) or get absorbed (in a room with lots of people, carpeting, drapes). It is advisable if you are purchasing a mic to try out a few models in the store to see how they color your voice.

If you are singing loudly and cannot be heard over the band, you cannot fix that by singing louder. Adjust the PA system, have the sound engineer (if there is one) work with you, and ask the band to play softer. Remember, you can only ask so much of your voice, whereas other instruments can adjust their volume levels. Everyone wants to keep their hearing intact, too! Watch Demonstration Video 27, "Microphone Technique."

▶

27

"SCREAM" SINGING OR GRITTY ROCK VOCALS

There is a skill to singing with a scream sound, such as used in many styles of metal music and hard rock. Scream singing can be produced softly, even though you may be squeezing your voice more than when you sing normally. Getting very close to a microphone will amplify you so you don't have to strain. Unfortunately, many people harm their voices with scream-singing. Seek out a teacher who really understands how to work with you safely if this is your goal.

For rock singers, a gritty sound is very common and even desirable, but often comes from vocal damage that the singer has accumulated over many years of vocal abuse and physical habits such as drugs, smoking, and drinking a lot of alcohol. (Why do we love the sound of a damaged voice? Why do we wish to *emulate* that sound?? I don't have the answer.) Occasionally, a person's voice is naturally gritty, but this is less common. Be *very* careful imitating a gritty tone when you're going for style. As mentioned earlier, you can introduce a small amount of *vocal fry*—occasionally—to add a gritty quality. Often the *false folds*, which are fleshy structures in your larynx that sit just above your "true" vocal folds, are being squeezed together to create this sound. That can be fatiguing, too. Use this approach judiciously. Remember to gauge whether or not you are tiring your voice based on how your voice feels. Does it get hoarse easily? Tire after singing? These are all indications that you are potentially hurting yourself. If you can sing gritty comfortably for two hours and have no ill effects, you're all set. Watch Demonstration Video 25, "Fry Voice and Intentional Gravel."

25

TIP: Going for High Notes

Bend your knees when you sing high notes. Remember, they're not really high! Don't think of singing them as reaching. Instead, going low in your body helps trick your mind to remember the notes are not high. It always works!

POWER

We've established that belting implies power. But being "powerful" when you sing can have different interpretations. A soft-spoken person can be very powerful, too. Think of some of the silver-screen villains who rarely raise their voices. Power comes from your intention. Your focus. When you focus your sound, similar to a light that is focused on a small point, it can carry a lot of intensity. Focus your thoughts when you sing, too. Add volume as you focus your performance intention, your sound, and your thoughts, and you will be formidable indeed. Power belting does not and should not always require over-the-top exertion. Belting can even be relatively easy—especially if you keep it moderately loud (rather than *fff*)—though athletically active, much of the time.

CHAPTER 4

The Healthy Belting Voice

Maintaining basic vocal wellness is important for singing in any style. You want to be especially mindful of how you use your voice whenever you belt. In this chapter, we'll take a look at good habits for a healthy belting voice, and point out warning signs that are indicators your vocal health could be at risk.

KEEP A LOG OF YOUR PRACTICE AND PROGRESS

Your body changes daily; so does your voice. For vocalists, it is important to learn how your voice responds to physical changes in your body, enabling you to gauge how your overall wellness impacts your singing. Keeping a daily log of your practice is very useful to get this information. It provides a baseline for what you can expect from your voice day to day, as well as detailed familiarity with cause-effect reasons that make singing easier or harder on a given day. Figure 4.1 is a practice log that you can use. Feel free to modify the log to fit your personal goals.

By keeping track of daily practice, you will notice patterns. Everyone has them. Observing your own patterns will give you a way to identify how you should expect your voice to work normally, based on your present skill level. This information also provides a basis of comparison for how your voice may change day to day. There are many things that can impact your belting: your sleep, diet, how you feel today overall on a scale of 1 to 10, how much time you spend practicing vocal technique, how much time you spend working on songs, how much you gig out and in what kind of venue, how loudly you speak, your stress level, and how easy or hard singing seems to be today overall. For example, what if the song you belted out effortlessly yesterday is really frustrating today? A daily practice log shows you what has changed, triggering fatigue or even strain. It shows you what you did (or didn't do) yesterday that made belting easier. This knowledge assists you in being mindful. Was your voice affected by something you ate? Did you work on a difficult passage for too long and tire out your voice? Did you practice a demanding vocal line without first warming up adequately? Did you push your voice through a sore throat, or in spite of fatigue from yesterday's gig? If your belting is going well today, did you drink more water? Get more sleep? Take adequate time warming up your voice first, so that it responded with flexibility and suppleness, before you shifted to belting? Blend non-belted songs into your set on the gig, and take breaks? Work with a PA system and instrumentation that supported you, so you could sing without shouting?

	Sleep Last Night	Today's Foods	How I Feel Today 1–10	Practice Time: When + hrs:mins	Technique/ Exercises I Practiced	Songs I Worked On	Stress Level Today 1–10	Ease of Singing Today 1–10	Recent Performance, Speaking, Yelling, Etc.
Monday									
Tuesday									
Wednesday									
Thursday									
Friday									
Saturday									
Sunday									

FIG. 4.1. Daily Practice Journal

KNOWING WHEN YOUR VOICE IS FINE

The truth is, unless you continually strain your voice (such as speaking with an under-supported fry voice, working a job with a very loud environment, or gigging frequently at loud venues), if your voice works normally, don't worry. Even when you belt frequently, if your voice does not tire or strain normally, you are probably okay. Most people have minor daily changes in the voice from such things as a head cold, monthly menses, or minor acid reflux. The body recovers. It's amazing that way.

To learn how your voice responds when it is healthy, get a scope by an expert *laryngologist*, a medical doctor who specializes in working with the voice. Major cities have voice centers with teams of doctors and voice therapists. The wellness visit provides an important baseline measurement of your "normal" voice as well as images of your actual vocal folds. Doctors are glad to have this data on file, as it provides them a personalized basis of comparison for your specific voice, should a problem arise. The doctor will likely also teach you tips and practices you should follow to keep your specific voice healthy. This is another significant benefit of a wellness visit.

A SOMATIC APPROACH TO BELTING

Originating from the Greek *somatikos*, meaning "belonging to the body," *somatics* is an approach originally developed in the 1970s by the philosopher Dr. Thomas Hanna to study how the body moves. Somatic awareness teaches you how your movements affect your experience. Feldenkrais, Alexander Technique, Rolfing, and Body Mapping are examples of somatic disciplines. In general, somatic awareness is helpful for gaining more understanding of what happens bodily when you sing, and what you can shift in your movements to improve performance. This is especially useful for belting.

> *"Somatic awareness teaches you how your movements affect your singing experience."*

Grounding and Your Feet

As singers, we tend to forget we have legs and feet! Too often, we sing only from the neck up. Our feet ground us. They hold us up. They balance us. When you are belting, it is doubly important to be grounded, so you don't strain your neck or your voice. Grounding helps you take deeper, more supporting breaths. If you feel unbalanced when you practice, perform, or audition, pay attention to your feet. Is your weight evenly distributed? Picture your balance distributed over three points on your feet: the ball of your foot behind your big toe, the ball of your foot behind your small toe, and your heel. Remember how much energy comes up to you through the ground. This awareness helps to alleviate neck tension, which is so prevalent among singers. It also helps manage anxiety that commonly comes along with performing and auditioning, such as stage fright.

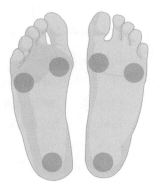

FIG. 4.2. Standing Points of Feet

If you're singing while seated at an instrument, you can still stay aware of your body's lower half and your posture from the hips up. Are you slouching at the piano? Leaning over a guitar? Reaching up to hit cymbals while twisting to sing into the mic? Or, are you thinking of being stable and strong from your core, free of tension at your instrument, comfortable in front of the mic? This awareness will make a tremendous difference in how your body responds to belting.

Use Movement to Belt, Both in Body and in Mind

Simply stated, sound is movement. Singing is movement. As we saw in chapter 2, music is made up of organized sound vibrations that we identify as tones and pleasing patterns. For singers, whose very bodies become the instruments making music, being aware of how we move is essential. Being aware of our thoughts, which direct our movements, is equally important.

Why, then, do so many singers stand stiffly in front of an audience? Perhaps in part, it is due to training. In some traditions, such as formal classical training, for example, singers are taught to minimize arm gestures and to streamline facial movements while achieving desired tones. Contemporary styles, on the other hand, which frequently include captivating rhythms and grooves, are less formal. Standing still or "properly" is not relevant. In fact, moving on stage helps express the meaning of the music and to engage the audience. This is especially true when you are belting. Quite often, the emotions you express are powerful, and movement helps to convey them. Movement also helps your breathing. (Watch Demonstration Video 28, "Use Your Arms," for more on this point.) Depending upon the specific style of music, how singers move will vary. Performances of rock or pop music are perhaps the most active on stage, while performances of jazz or folk are often generally less so. If you are accustomed to singing in a style that has less movement on stage, experiment with adding movements to free you for belting.

28

Your own personality is important to consider, too. If you are naturally a quiet person, being very active on stage may seem inauthentic. If you are naturally very energetic, your performance can become a focused opportunity for self-expression. One good way to find out if you are moving, stiff, or all-over-the-place is to videotape yourself. The camera won't lie. Watch and find out!

Fear of being judged usually makes us behave differently in front of other people. Less-experienced singers frequently hold still on stage, feeling exposed and vulnerable. It may even seem as if people in the audience are able to see into your very soul! Or, the opposite can happen instead: a singer jumps around excessively, pushing belted vocals out with exuberance and deep knee bends, possibly to compensate for the fear of sounding *under*whelming. (For more on this point see chapter 3, "Myth 2.")

Physical movements are essential to help you stay relaxed and engaged. Mental movements—staying awake, and mindful—are also indispensible. They enhance your concentration while you sing, and heighten your awareness. You are able to keep track of several aspects of a performance at once, without becoming overwhelmed. You hear the groove of the band, you see the stage lights, and you know the best place to stand. You see silhouettes of people in the audience as you align your gestures with the music as if in a dance. You hear and see your band's cues and witness their immersion in the music. You hear venue sounds such as the rustling of dishes and glasses, clapping hands, people calling out. You recall your lyrics, and you think of something poignant to say before you begin the next song. You plant your feet and feel the ground supporting you as you take in a deep, calm breath before you go for a loud, high belted note. While all of this is happening, you observe how each song affects you, and how that impacts your emotional connection to the next song in the set. You observe how the set affects your expectations of what you are about to sing or say next. You learn to hold all of these things at once within the larger wholeness of your Self, as a beautiful earthen vessel can hold water that supports several tea lights floating on top, effortlessly.

Stay Active

Remember, your entire body is cooperating with you to get the job done. Sound is movement. Singing is movement. If you hold yourself too stiffly, many muscles that are not needed for singing will be too contracted and keep you tense. Keep moving! Use the natural flow of movement to energize yourself. Move your arms around as you practice, explore your space. Go low, go high.

Human beings are designed to move. When we are active and fit we are more able to use our whole selves to belt at our best. Do you work out? It is not reasonable to expect your breath will be deep and athletic for belting if you do not. So, take walks to activate your lung capacity. Or go to the gym. Dance. Rock climb. Hike. Ride a bike. Lift weights. (Keep hydrated during activity, too.) Do something—anything physically active that you enjoy—regularly.

Know What Is in Front of You, What Is Behind You

Part of awareness is remembering that we occupy space in several directions. Movement occurs not only in front of us; it is all around us, too. Because our eyes focus forward, because we walk forward, because our arms reach forward, we lean our heavy heads down to touch something in front of us. Because our voices project forward from the mouth, we speak to the person who is in front of us. When we perform, we face the audience seated in front of us, while other musicians on stage are usually behind the singer, or to the side. This makes it easy to forget about what is behind us.

FIG. 4.3. Spatial Awareness

A common problem for singers is forgetting that the body takes up three-dimensional space. When you focus only on your voice, the rest of the body below the neck is forgotten. Yet your voice travels all around you. You have a back and legs, and arms that can move in nearly 360 degrees. Keeping back muscles strengthened not only helps posture, it also supports deeper breathing that is essential for belting. The energy surrounding you is like a fluid, crystal sphere. Staying aware of this 360-degree sphere of energy will make your belting more effortless. It is possible to adjust mindfulness to include this energy and your movements that are behind you (though you can't see them), as well as in front (where you can see). It just requires awareness, and gentle reminders to yourself to "look." Then, when you sing with awareness of the sound surrounding you, tension in the larynx will diminish. This awareness also makes you more formidable and commanding in performance.

HOW CAN I BELT WITHOUT HARMING MY VOICE?

We are all different. I've seen name-brand artists belt with noticeable tension in their jaws—which frequently leads to vocal strain for most people—and yet continue to do so throughout a decades-long career. Any vocal medical expert will tell you that this is unusual. Therefore, it is essential that you learn your own physical strengths and weaknesses. Don't assume that if you imitate how a famous person belts, you'll sound like that person and never have vocal issues. Below are very common topics that come up in the voice lesson, and how to address them.

Common Problems and Solutions for Belters

Using 100 Percent Chest Voice

As we discussed in chapter 3, many singers and teachers alike believe that belting means using all chest voice. Although chest voice is fine for lower notes, you don't want to power it up all the way to your "break." You may be able to use your chest voice higher in your range for an isolated phrase here and there (such as within a melismatic riff), but continually pushing up your chest voice is never a good recipe. In fact, once you get past the chest voice myth, you might even stop worrying about your break altogether! Remember, continually pushing up against the top boundaries of your chest voice creates two undesirable results:

1. It trains your belting to be limited to using *only* chest voice, making any notes that sit above the top of this range difficult or even impossible to use.

2. The all-powerful, all-flexible, all-awesome mix voice technique is eliminated from your tonal palette.

The solution? Learn to use your mix voice! First step: sing *lighter* as you ascend in pitch. Work with the exercises provided in part II to practice this strategy.

High Voices Are More Susceptible to Injury Than Low Voices

When you sing high-pitched notes, your vocal folds come together many more times per second than when you sing lower notes. Then, because singing in a belt voice is forceful, it increases the impact velocity of the vocal folds each time they come together (hundreds of times per second). This means that women's voices, whose notes are normally higher than men's, endure this impact more frequently. This makes women more susceptible to problems arising from big singing.

The solution? Be mindful of how you belt! Be sure to follow the healthy-singing guidelines throughout this book.

If It Hurts or Strains, Stop!

Issues such as vocal fatigue, strain, swelling, or nodules come from overuse and abuse. If your voice is tired or feels strained after you belt, rest it. If it is more difficult to speak after you sing, change how you sing those songs. You have been overdoing it.

Sometimes, there is a medical reason why your voice becomes fatigued or swollen. Asthma, some medications, and getting over an illness like a cold or flu will all cause your vocal folds to swell. This is decidedly *not* the time to push your voice. Be careful. Sing lightly; that movement may help the swelling to go down. But don't belt.

Pushing through vocal fatigue or strain is a bad idea that can potentially harm your voice. Why? Unlike large muscles such as those in your arms and legs, the vocal folds themselves are not muscles at all and cannot sustain excessive use. Instead, they are delicate *membranes* that stretch over ligaments that attach to muscle. The folds will weaken, swell, and worse, if you push them too hard!

Minimizing Tension

Whenever you belt, there is increased force and tension applied to the voice. It is unavoidable: singing with zero tension is impossible, because muscles have to tense (contract) in order to produce any kind of movement. Singers, however, too often overly contract muscles that are not needed for belting, which in turn makes muscles around the voice too tight. This is why relaxing as many parts of your body as possible (while still maintaining good posture and breath support, of course) when you belt is especially important. Are you squeezing your voice or tightening your upper chest and shoulders? This only increases the likelihood of potential vocal problems. Is your jaw loose, or are you in the habit of "doing the Muppet" (jaw bouncing up and down) with every note in a run? Exercise your jaw to teach it to relax when you sing. Are you clenching your fists? Release your hands. Are your toes curled? Be aware of your feet. Are you gripping your abdominal muscles to increase your breath support? You can support your inhaled breath calmly with your upper abs. There's no need to work like crazy to breathe in.

Power Is in a Balanced Breath

As we saw in chapter 2, your breath is the true powerhouse for belting. A powerful, directed breath comes from core abdominal *balance* and from regular, calm singing practice. As you prepare to sing a note, be sure your breaths are lower in the body and at ease on inhalation, then supported on exhalation with a *small* contraction of your upper abs. This will help to keep the air in your lungs longer. Moving your arms when you sing also helps you experience the sensation of supported breathing. (Refer back to Demonstration Video 28, "Use

Your Arms.") Remember, gripping your abs tight won't make your breathing stronger or more supported, and in fact can have the opposite effect by making the body too tense.

28

Open Vocal Tract

The more you utilize the resonant space in your mouth when you belt, the more you can relax squeezing and constriction in your vocal tract (areas of your pharynx and larynx). Visualize space in your mouth whenever you belt, especially as you ascend in pitch. This will help your voice to last.

Diction

Diction—how you pronounce words—has a big impact on how you belt. When you sing lower in your range, you are able to pronounce words pretty closely to how you would normally speak them. However, when you belt higher notes your diction needs to change some to compensate for the increased pressure on your voice. Vowel sounds need to open up, and each word's closing consonant should be articulated *at the end* of the note or phrase.

Here's how: First, focus on singing the vowel of the word you are belting. If the word contains a diphthong (two or more vowel sounds blended together— refer back to chapter 3, "Get More Sound with Less Work"), emphasize the most *relaxed* part of the word as you sing it. There is no exact rule for this; experiment in your own mouth to find which vowel sound sings the most freely on any given pitch. For example, depending on the melody, the two-syllable word "baby" is often sung like this: "Ba...y-beeee," or even, "Ba...y-ba...y!" Second, wait to articulate the closing consonant until you are done singing the note. This strategy keeps your mouth open for more sound, and helps keep it from over-tightening. For example, "Please wait!" would be sung "plEEE...se-wA...eeT!" rather than "PLeeZZZ WHayeeTT." See exercise 12 in part II for practicing long and short vowel sounds.

Getting It Looked At Professionally

As we discussed in chapter 3, knowing what your neutral, healthy voice looks and behaves like is very important. Singers too often wait until there is a serious problem before visiting the *laryngologist,* a doctor who specializes in vocal medicine. Because many vocal issues can be triggered by two or three causes, it may be impossible for a voice teacher to really know the reason you are having an issue simply by listening to you sing. The best way to learn what is actually going on inside your voice is by having it looked at by the doctor. He or she will use a medical vocal scope and video imagery to take a detailed look at your vocal folds. If you do experience a problem, don't wait to see the doctor to get it checked out; and, in the meantime, take it easy.

WELLNESS HABITS FOR THE SINGER

Staying Hydrated

Being well hydrated is important not only for your overall health, it is essential for your voice to function properly. Drinking water regularly throughout the day helps to maintain the mucosal layer on your vocal folds, which is essential for your voice to work well. This is especially vital for belting, because dry vocal folds can be seriously harmed when coming together with the force of big singing. The standard medical recommendation is to drink a minimum of six to eight eight-ounce glasses of water a day. Carry a water bottle with you to work or school, sipping on it throughout the day, refill as needed. "Drink often, pee pale." Drinking water will also help to rinse away any mucous on the back of your throat that can trickle down onto your voice and gum up the works.

Remember, you cannot moisten your vocal folds directly by drinking water or tea. This is because the vocal folds are the gateway to your lungs, located beneath the epiglottis cartilage in your larynx that folds down when you swallow. (If liquid could go onto your voice it would flow into your lungs, not down your throat.) One way you *can* moisten your vocal folds directly is to breathe in steam, either in the shower or with a (clean) vapor inhaler, available at the drugstore. A good general rule of thumb is to keep sipping fluids so you never feel extremely thirsty. This will keep your body's cells well hydrated, and in turn your voice will be, too.

Stabilizing Your Everyday Breathing

These days, we are so stressed all the time, our bodies are in a chronic state of high alert. We often forget just to *breathe*, to move more slowly, to experience calm. Belting is so high-energy that it often comes along with high stress, too. To practice remedying this habitual state, try this now: Take a moment. Breathe in slowly for four counts, picturing your midsection filling naturally. Now, hold your breath for four counts, then exhale for eight counts. Observe whether there are parts in your body that are tense, and allow them to release. Close your eyes. Repeat until relaxed. ☺

Slow, deep breathing helps neutralize the release of the stress hormones adrenaline and cortisol into your blood stream when you are nervous or tense. These two hormones are part of the sympathetic nervous system's "fight or flight" response, which is designed to protect you from harm. These hormones also tense your muscles in readiness for escape (from a crazy wild lion, for example).

If you stop regularly throughout your day for a few minutes to simply *breathe*, encouraging peaceful stillness while you do, your overall stress level will decrease. You can practice this anywhere, even in a crowded place such as on a bus or waiting in line. Then, when you belt, your breathing will already be in the habit of being low in the belly and calm. In this way, deep, supported breathing will always be accessible to you.

Taking Care of Your Speaking Voice

You use your voice all day long to speak. It is the same instrument as your singing voice. Are you mindful of how you speak? Do you give yourself adequate breath support for talking? Most vocal fatigue and strain result from how we speak. Lazy, under-supported speaking such as vocal fry is one common culprit. So is squeezing your throat to project your voice, without having first taken in a good breath. For vocal fry, try speaking one to two pitches higher than normal, to lift your voice out of this fatiguing placement. It might sound weird to you at first, but chances are no one else will notice such a small change. If you are a tense talker, breathe before you speak! (Refer back to Demonstration Video 25, "Fry Voice and Intentional Gravel.")

25

Smoking

Smoking—anything—dries out your voice. When your voice is dry, it chafes. When it chafes, it can become injured. Smoking also damages your lungs, limiting how deeply you are able to breathe in. You need full, sustaining breaths to belt well, in addition to well-hydrated, flexible vocal folds.

Some singers believe that smoking will give them the popular "raspy" sound we hear so often these days, especially in belted-out rock vocals. Why does smoking make the voice raspy? It has become damaged. It's become roughed up, like two pieces of sandpaper rubbing together. This is permanent damage that makes it progressively difficult to produce sound. There are better ways to get the sound you like. If you value your voice, be disciplined. Don't smoke.

Foods and Medicines

Everyone is different when it comes to what foods are okay to eat and what foods should be avoided before you sing. When you keep your daily practice log, notice if you see any connection between what you eat and how easy or difficult it is to sing. You may notice a specific food makes singing more difficult. On the other hand, you may not be affected by foods at all. You know best. Here are some general guidelines to help you.

Caffeine

Drinks with caffeine like coffee, tea, and soft drinks cause your body to flush fluids out of your cells. If you drink caffeinated beverages, compensate with additional water. Caffeine can also cause constriction of blood vessels throughout your body (that's why it's put into wrinkle cream), a real problem for belters. You may find your voice feels tighter if you sing right after having caffeine. If so, allow several hours in-between a cup of coffee or soda and when you sing, because caffeine stays in your system for six to eight hours or longer. You definitely do *not* want to belt with a voice that has been tightened from caffeine. Coffee may also create excess mucous due to properties of the coffee bean, separate from caffeine.

Dairy and Chocolate

Some people find dairy products such as milk or yogurt cause thickened mucus on the voice. Thickened mucus affects how your vocal folds vibrate together, usually making singing more difficult. Just to be on the safe side, avoid any dairy within a few hours of belting.

In spite of rumors to the contrary, there is no medical proof that chocolate is bad for your voice. Again, learn your own body's reaction to foods like chocolate.

Reflux

If you notice a correlation between a specific food and stomach upset, the lining of your stomach could be irritated and causing gastric reflux (heartburn). Even when your throat doesn't burn, silent gastric reflux can irritate the tissues in your throat and larynx. This causes swelling and mucous there, which makes singing more difficult. The best way to find out for sure is to be seen by an ear, nose, and throat doctor or by a laryngologist.

Medicines

Many commonly prescribed medicines dry out the voice, although most doctors are unaware of this side effect unless they specialize in vocal medicine. Asthma discs, antihistamines, and decongestants are just some examples of medicines that dry the vocal folds. You should research medicines you take in order to learn if they affect your voice.[7] If you discover a connection, ask your doctor to work with you to find an alternate medicine that is not drying.

If you have a head cold or allergies, take it especially easy with belting. Weigh the benefits of being symptom-free from over-the-counter medicines, against the downsides of drying out. Be proactive for your health.

---

7. One useful website for researching how medicines affect the voice is
   www.entnet.org/HealthInformation/medsVoice.cfm

Throat Clearing

When you need to clear your throat, do so gently. Every time you make a harsh sound to clear your throat—although it may feel satisfying—you are hammering your vocal folds together!

If you clear your throat frequently, you may have thickened mucus in your throat that feels like something is stuck there. Are you drinking enough water? If yes, visit your doctor to address what might be causing the problem.

Thoughts and Beliefs

Your singing voice responds 100 percent to your thoughts, both conscious and unconscious. Every habit you have learned started out as a thought. We gain skill and coordination for a physical activity like belting with repetition, including habits that either assist or interfere with your goal. When you practice something repeatedly, it becomes an unconscious behavior.

Your voice is part of *you*. People identify very personally and sensitively with how they sound. It is only natural to be uncomfortable singing in front of other people. We feel exposed, vulnerable, judged, even at risk. When we are uncomfortable, we may either pull inward to protect ourselves, or push outward in self-defense. If you are feeling this way and you get up to belt, part of you is singing outwardly in a big, dramatic way—while another part is guarding you from perceived danger. This causes your muscles to over-contract in self-protection, and makes belting very difficult, definitely strained, and even harmful to your voice.

Therefore, practice mindfulness. Learn to recognize your beliefs. Are they legitimate, or are they fears you can manage that pull you away from your goal?

Examine what you believe about belting. Is it bad for you? Or, is belting a singing approach to use for heightened moments of expression and power? Should belting always be hard? Or, is belting a way to sing that, although it may be somewhat strenuous, should not hurt your voice? If you think it will be difficult to belt, your body will comply and make it hard. Remember, you have to practice. You cannot get good at anything simply by reading about it. Take things slowly as you get started. Follow these tips and guidelines and you should be well on your way to a healthy belting voice.

All right, enough talk! Let's get singing! Turn the page to head on into part II, Exercises for Belting. Use the online audio tracks to practice with. Please be sure to watch the online videos, too.

PART II

EXERCISES FOR BELTING

These exercises will help you develop your belting technique. Be sure to practice with the audio files that accompany these exercises and watch the how-to videos, available at www.halleonard.com/mylibrary. To access them, enter the code found on the first page of this book.

All of the exercises provide a recommended starting key or pitch. However, as each voice is unique, you may wish to move your starting note up or down a step or two. That is perfectly okay. The audio accompaniment files provide a range of keys in which to sing the exercises, though you may also modulate beyond what's notated or recorded when you practice them on your own. Once your voice is adequately warmed up, you may also wish to practice the exercises moving a little higher or lower in pitch than written. In other words, you do not need to limit yourself to the exact pitches provided here. The response of your voice will let you know what range of pitches suit it best for each exercise. For exercises marked "Continue, ascending," keep repeating the exercise, ascending by half steps, until you reach a comfortable top. (Don't push it past comfort.) Then, return back down and travel a bit below where you started.

The exercises begin with basic breathing to get you grounded and ready to produce big singing without straining. Then, we move into easy sung exercises to get you warmed up. Next, we work on exercises for belting after you're warmed up and flexible. Finally, as the exercises progress in difficulty, you work on range, melody, and intervallic jumps around register shifts. To demonstrate variety, the four singers in the videos provide different voices belting many of the exercises.

1

EXERCISE 1. BREATH EXERCISE 1: HISSING

This exercise teaches you to breathe in calmly, pause, and then produce a pressured sound on a hiss (SSS) with increasingly shortened inhalations. This exercise supports the discussion of breathing in chapter 3.

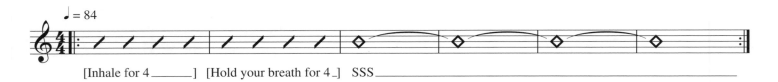

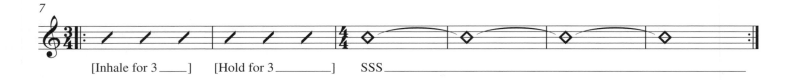

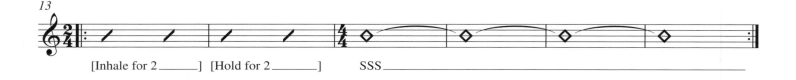

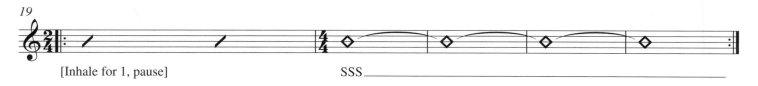

FIG. II.1. Breath Exercise 1

Variation

Introducing a simple yoga exercise will help you stabilize both your posture and your breathing without becoming overly tense. Stand on one foot (preferably not while wearing heels), with the other leg bent at the knee. Find your balance. How are you standing on one foot? Some muscles are contracted or you would fall down, but if you are too tense, you cannot balance. Once you feel stable, repeat the exercise.

EXERCISE 2. PULSING FOR BREATH MANAGEMENT

Use this exercise to practice abdominal-supported breathing. The exercise repeats five notes on one breath: four pulses and then one held note. The pulses should sound almost grunt-like, with a non-breath break in between them.

Start the exercise by planting your feet solidly, with soft knees. Take in a deep, low breath. Then, as you phonate each pulsed note, you should notice your abdomen contracting slightly inward. This is the action of your diaphragm muscle pushing out air. Breathe as indicated by the checkmarks. The first time you do the exercise, use a "neutral" tone. Then, repeat the entire exercise using a chest voice tone. Finally, transpose the exercise to notes that are higher in your range, using a mix-voice tone as described in chapters 2 and 3.

3 – 5   2

Higher Voices

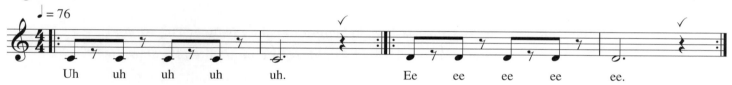

Lower Voices

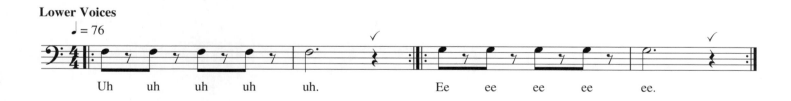

FIG. II.2. Pulsing for Breath Control

EXERCISE 3. BREATH SUPPORT: SINGING *AH* AND *EE* ON A HELD NOTE

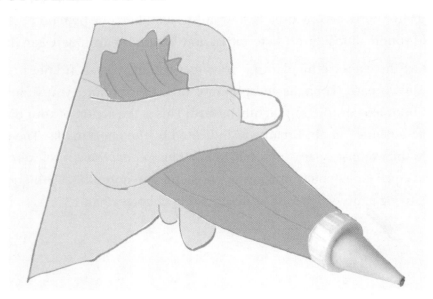

FIG. II.3.1. Squeezing an Icing Tube

Steady airflow is an essential basic ingredient for healthy belting. This exercise trains you to maintain steady airflow by holding one long note at a constant volume. When you begin to sing the note you will feel full with the air you just inhaled. It is natural to use up a lot of air then, but resist this temptation. Instead, hold back some of the air when you begin to sing, which leaves some air available to press up from your abdomen (if needed) toward the end of the note. This will help to keep the volume consistent. It's as if you're painting a line of icing across a cake: you want the line to be even, not globby. If you press too hard on the icing tube, it will come gushing out; too little, and your line will have gaps in it (see figure II.3.1). Instead, by using steady pressure that increases gradually as the content decreases, the icing—and your airflow—will remain constant.

You can play around with different notes when you practice this. The pitches are less important than the experience of a breath that supports a steady, clear tone that is also free and easy.

6 – 7   3

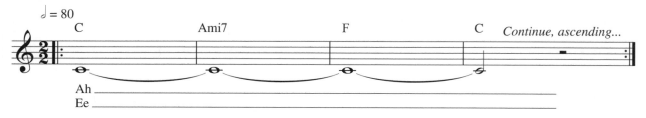

FIG. II.3.2. Singing Ah and Ee on a Held Note

EXERCISE 4. BEGIN BELTING WITHOUT TENSION

This is a way to use a belt tone while gliding between notes a whole step apart. The exercise takes you through a short range of a fourth while trying out different vowels. If a vowel seems too tight and causes any strain, stop! Change the vowel. What is important with this exercise is to glide between notes and blend them together, like a violin—not a piano. (You can watch an example of how vowel shapes change the way you sound in Video 4: "Begin Belting without Tension")

8 – 10   4

FIG. II.4. Begin Belting

EXERCISE 5. CLEAN "NEUTRAL" TONES, USING CHROMATICS

A series of chromatic notes provides all the pitches available in the western twelve-note scale. By singing chromatics in a clean, neutral tone, you are compelled to embrace every pitch within a range of notes. Your voice will shift and move depending on where a note sits in your voice and on its vowel shape. Learning to embrace every note, with flexibility rather than using force, you will enhance your fine motor control, which is essential for belting mix tones. If the exercise gets too high or uncomfortable, stop. Don't push it.

11 – 12   5

FIG. II.5. Clean Neutral Tones Using Chromatics

EXERCISE 6. CRESCENDO AND DECRESCENDO: *AH*

In this exercise, you begin holding one note very softly. Then, while still on the same breath, crescendo to a loud belt tone. Next, take a new breath and begin singing the same note in a loud belt, then decrescendo as you continue to hold the note until it is again very soft.

As you crescendo or decrescendo, it is typical to reach a point at which you feel your voice wants to change gears. The approaching change may even feel abrupt, causing you to try to avoid it. Don't avoid it! Embrace it. Some singers find the change is more obvious as they *crescendo*, while for others it is during the *decrescendo* that they really notice it. Either way, you *will* notice a physical change in your voice, especially on higher pitches. You will likely hear your tone change at that moment, too. Many singers think of this as a change in registers, a break, or as navigating through the *passaggio*. It is essential to take your time during that moment. Go as slowly as possible, as if you are examining every fiber of this transition and observing its elasticity. Let it sound bad if necessary, in order to learn to smooth this area out. This practice teaches you to shift between different shapes of your vocal folds without having to lurch or skip over areas of your voice. In this way, you learn strategies to *navigate* changes in your voice, and may even find ultimately that your registers blend together seamlessly.

13 – 15   6

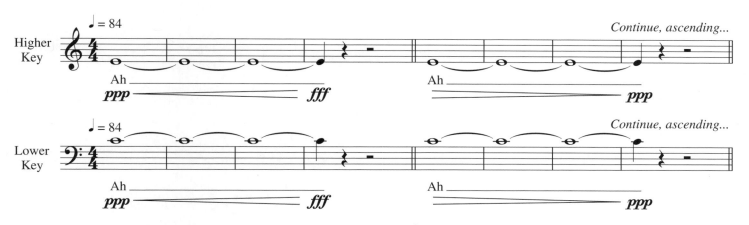

FIG. II.6a. Crescendo and Decrescendo on "Ah"

Variation: Crescendo and Decrescendo: *Ee*

Following the same procedure as in exercise 6a, this variation practices using a bright, "forward" mix tone rather than a pressed chest voice. Notice that the vowel "Ee" opens up to "Eeh" as you crescendo on the note. This is very important in order to avoid straining. Baritones may wish to begin the exercise a whole step lower if you find that you are having to flip in and out of *falsetto*.

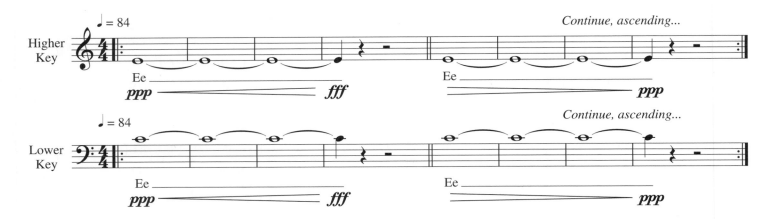

FIG. II.6b. Crescendo and Decrescendo on "Ee." Continue ascending into mix and falsetto, while avoiding straining.

EXERCISE 7. DEVELOPING MIX VOICE

This exercise uses a simple scale down from Sol to Do (5 to 1) on three separate vowels. Begin on A in the middle of your range, gliding through the notes so they connect. Then, work your way up through key changes by half steps or whole steps. Keep the tone clean and *mf*, but never get crazy-loud. You can try out other vowels too, to see which ones glide the most effortlessly. This will help you to develop and strengthen your mix voice.

17 – 19   7

FIG. II.7a. Developing Mix Voice

*Visualization suggestion for this exercise: When you begin the exercise on a note that is relatively high in your range, do this before you sing:

1. Take in a calm, full, low breath.

2. Pause as you prepare to sing by holding your breath for a brief moment. It's as if your body is a bottle holding ample air and has a gentle cork keeping the air in place.

3. As you pause, hear the note you will be singing in your mind, along with the connectedness of the five-note sequence.

4. Release the air (without force or popping) as you begin to sing.

Variation: Singing "Mia"

Singing "mia" takes you through a diphthong with two sounds on each pitch, "mi" and "uh" as well as the beginning consonant "m." This addition of sounds makes the exercise a bit more challenging. The notes printed here take you through three keys. Continue up the scale, then sing back down to end where you started.

20 – 22   7

FIG. II.7b. Variation "Mia"

EXERCISE 8. EXPLORING OVERTONES

In this exercise, you roll vowels forward in your mouth while holding a note, in order to manipulate the overtones (or harmonics) in your tone. You will hear your sound change as you do this. Begin singing a bright Ee vowel, which sits roughly in the middle of your hard palate (the roof of your mouth). Press the sound against the hard palate as you roll it forward—slowly—with the flat part of your tongue, through the vowels Ee, Eu, Oo, and Er. End the roll on a hard Rrr sound (like imitating a pirate). Try rolling back and forth between Rrr and Er. You should start to hear a high frequency moving and shifting above the note you are holding.

Exaggerating higher frequencies in your tone is a very useful way to build a strong belted mix sound. Please refer to the video demonstration to observe how this is done.[8]

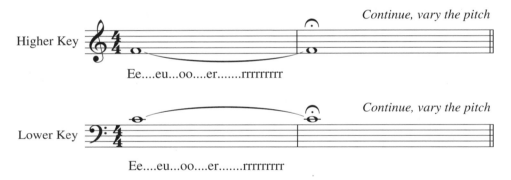

FIG. II.8. Exploring Overtones

---

8. If you're interested in learning more about singing overtones, check out Tuvan throat singing, a form of overtone singing by people from Mongolia and Tuva. It is amazing to watch and easy to find on the Web.

EXERCISE 9. BELTED "SIREN"

Belters often leap up intervals of a fifth or an octave to peak on a high, exciting note. To condition this leap in a way that is powerful, yet flexible and versatile—and does not strain your voice—this exercise adapts the classic siren exercise. Sirens are a wonderful way to glide through all the pivots and shifts in your voice on a *glissando*. To belt a siren, follow these steps:

1. Begin singing in chest or full voice on the low note.

2. As you glide up to the octave, allow your voice to shift into mix placement while keeping the sound loud. Mix placement will feel somewhat lighter, perhaps thinner, but is still amply loud especially when it is placed forward in the mouth. Avoid flipping into head voice.

3. Still on the same breath, glide back down to the starting note and allow the sound to press back into chest or full voice.

25 – 26   9

FIG. II.9. Siren Exercise

EXERCISE 10. GLISSANDO THROUGH YOUR "BREAK" INTO MIX

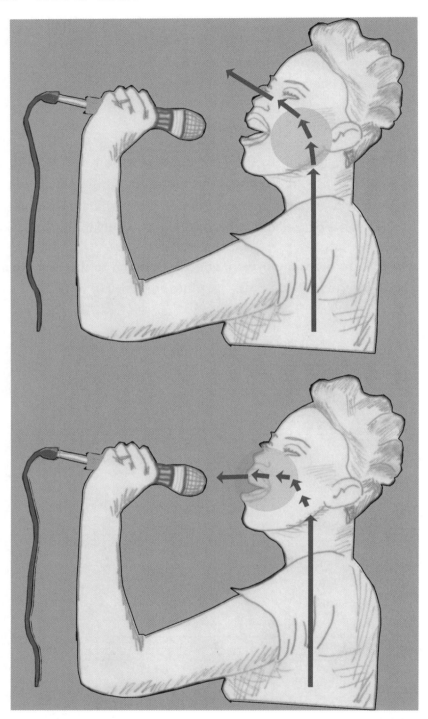

FIG. II.10.1. Placing "C@t." Sound rotates forward in the mouth as pitch ascends. Top: Sound should not feel like it goes "up," nor come from the back of your throat. Bottom: Instead, sound travels forward and out.

This exercise uses a *glissando* on a very bright "@" (aah) sound, as in the word "cat." The exercise encourages you to blend tones together while your larynx shifts to sing different notes within one phrase. It's like swirling your fingers on a charcoal drawing to blend the colors together. Your tone begins full on the bottom, then gradually lightens—ideally without breaking or flipping—as you ascend up through the glissando. Sometimes, you may find your voice wanting to shift into falsetto (men) or head voice (women) to reach the top octave note. You can experiment with allowing that to happen, as long as you do not *let go* of the physical sensation of staying connected to the notes as they transition within your voice. Alternatively, let mix voice take over the top octave. Here is a helpful visualization for this: With each note that you ascend to, the sound rotates forward in your mouth to become brighter and slightly thinner. Be careful that you don't pull the sound back in your mouth as you ascend, illustrated in figure II.10.1. This usually causes unnecessary vocal tension and can lead you to strain. High tenors may wish to explore higher mix notes before transitioning into pure falsetto.

27 – 28   10

FIG. II.10.2. C @t Exercise

EXERCISE 11. TRANSITIONING THROUGH YOUR "BREAK": MAJOR/MINOR

Work on this exercise once you are warmed up and have become more flexible shifting into mix voice. This exercise takes you through a glissando similar to exercise 10, with the addition of the subtle shift within a triad between the major and minor thirds. The keys selected here begin at the usual transition point for women between chest voice and a lighter tone, and for men approaching falsetto at the top note of the exercise. Keep the tone consistent, but lighten it somewhat as you reach the fifth (Sol). In some cases, you may not need to change your tone at all, depending upon your individual voice. Once you are familiar with this exercise, try it one to two steps higher to expand your range. Always be sure your singing stays comfortable. Male voices may continue to modulate the exercise into falsetto; female voices should find the provided range adequate to practice belt tones in chest and mix voice.

29 – 31   11

FIG. II.11. Transitioning through a Break: Major/Minor. Male voices only should continue modulating.

EXERCISE 12. BELTING LONG AND SHORT SOUNDS

This exercise puts long and short belted sounds together within one phrase, while singing the notes of a major triad with a dominant seventh. The inside of your mouth should be open and lifted in the back, and the jaw dropped, to allow for maximum resonant space with the least amount of tightening. Be sure you are well warmed up before singing this exercise. Repeat this exercise, transposing it up a half step each time, or starting on different notes.

32 – 33   12

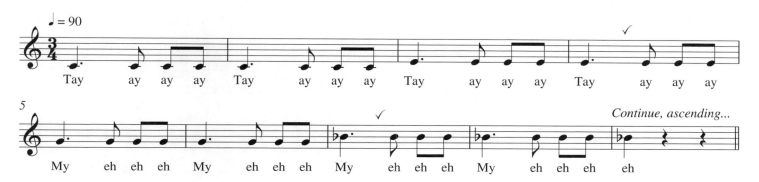

FIG. II.12. Belting Long and Short Sounds

EXERCISE 13. ARPEGGIATED SCALE TO BLEND REGISTERS

This exercise shows you how to blend registers while belting from a loud, low tone into a high, mix tone. The important strategy for this exercise is *lightening* as you ascend while imagining the notes are rotating slightly forward in your mouth; then, as you descend back to Do (1), allow your voice to fill in again. This approach will take you in and out of mix voice. Be very mindful not to push your chest voice all the way up, nor to sing only in head voice (as you would if you were just starting to warm up). Experiment with different vowels, and keys, higher and lower.

34 – 35   13

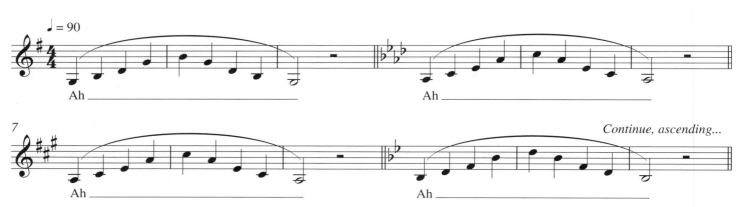

FIG. II.13a. Arpeggiated Scale to Blend Registers

Variation

The classic arpeggiated scale up to the ninth then back down, sung on a bright "ah" vowel.

36 – 37   13

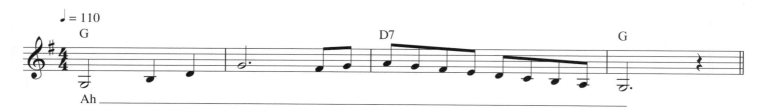

FIG. II.13b. Arpeggiated Scale to Blend Registers Variation

EXERCISE 14. BELT MELODY 1: MIXING TONES

This melody carries you through a variety of tones and registers. Please refer to the video and audio examples to hear the phrasing and where vocal placement shifts in the demonstrations. However, as your voice is unique, you may very likely wish (or need) to sing the example somewhat differently from how it is demonstrated here. Experiment with different keys, higher and lower.

FIG. II.14. Belt Melody 1

EXERCISE 15. BELT MELODY 2: RELAXED JAW

Whenever you sing high, strong phrases, be especially mindful if your jaw tends to reach upwards or open agape like a crocodile's. It is a very common occurrence that even pop stars demonstrate, but tensing your jaw in this way will not help you to sing any better. It only makes singing harder and more prone to strain. Instead, if a note feels high—try bending your knees as you approach it. If you have a lower vocal type, you can also lower the key until you are comfortable with the exercise, then attempt it as written. You may also try this exercise on different vowel sounds, or make up your own lyrics. Experiment with different keys, higher and lower.

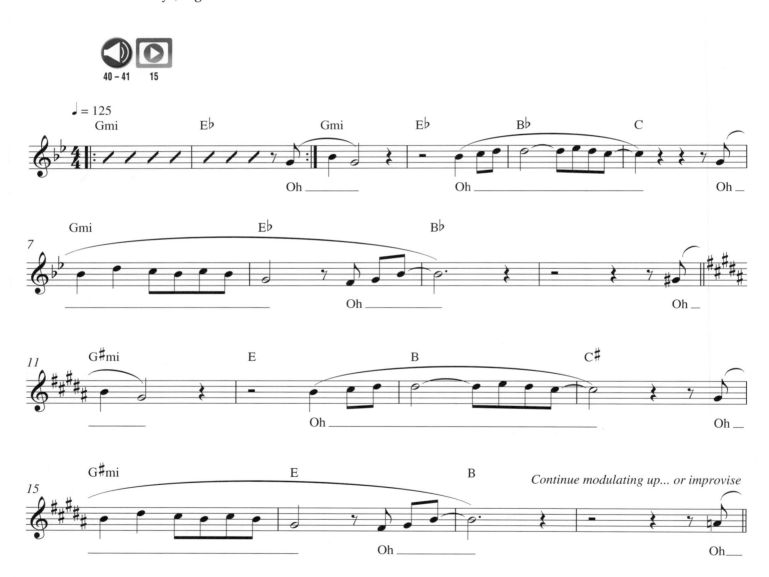

FIG. II.15. Belt Melody 2

EXERCISE 16. BELT MELODY 3: POP BALLAD

This melody uses a very open "Oh" vowel. However, some people find "Ee" or "Oo" less straining to belt than "Oh." If that describes you, go ahead and modify the vowel. Ultimately, whenever you belt a melody with lyrics, you adjust a word's vowel to widen it as the melody ascends. It is also important to avoid belting out a diphthong (discussed in chapters 3 and 4). Sometimes, you may even need to adjust a vowel to a placement in your mouth that is more effortless for you. Experiment with this. Experiment with different keys, higher and lower.

FIG. II.16. Belt Melody 3

EXERCISE 17. BELT MELODY 4: POP BALLAD

This exercise is a melody with a good range, legato lines, and open vowels. Experiment with singing it using louder and softer belting tones. Below are higher and lower keys, along with an alternate melody line that is more dramatic (and more difficult). Experiment with different keys, higher and lower.

44 – 46   17

Higher Key

FIG. II.17a. Belt Melody 4: Higher Key

Lower Key

FIG. II.17b. Belt Melody 4: Lower Key

Variation: Alternate Melody

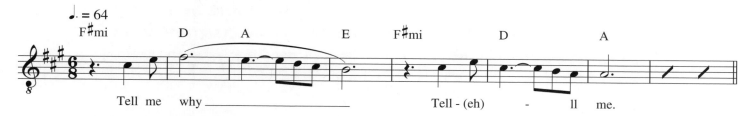

FIG. II.17c. Belt Melody 4: Variation

EXERCISE 18. 12-BAR BLUES MELODY IN C

These practice melodies are in a 12-bar blues style. Please watch the video, and try out the audio sing-along to practice them. If the key doesn't fit your voice like a glove, feel free to change it. Experiment with different keys, higher and lower.

47 – 48   18

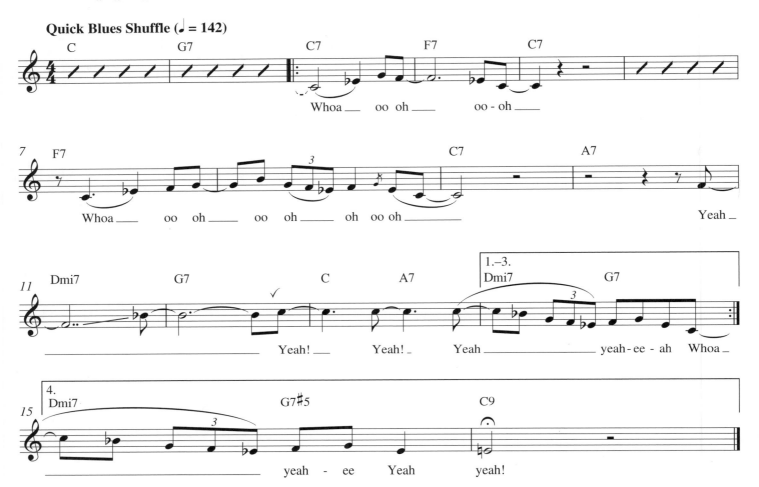

FIG. II.18a. 12-Bar Blues Melody in C

Variation

FIG. II.18b. 12-Bar Blues Melody in C: Variation

EXERCISE 19. POP-ROCK UP-TEMPO BELT MELODY

This mini-song has lots of opportunity for you to experiment with your belted riffs. The melody provided can be varied somewhat as you explore your own interpretational style, vocal range, and flexibility. The ending vamp is open for you to take some chances! Experiment with different keys, higher and lower.

49 – 51   19

Straight 8th Rock Feel (♩ = 142)

Just one tick-et a - way _____ boy, ___ a - way ___ Bought my tick-et to - day __

Watch me make it

You told __ me ___ that you love __ me I do be - lieve __

You teach __ me, know how ___ to drive __ me __ cra - zy. ___ One tick-et a - way __

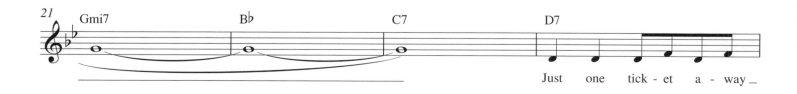

Just one tick-et a - way __

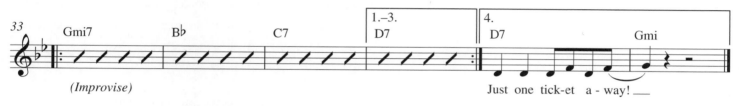

FIG. II.19. Pop-Rock Up-Tempo Melody

EXERCISE 20. POP-R&B MELODY

In this short melody, work on blending belting and non-belting to create a variety of colors and textures in your singing. Experiment with different keys, higher and lower.

52 – 54   20

Right,   right at the start, __   o-pen your heart, __   to see all the love __

__   I've   got you in   mind, __   shar-ing my   days, __   shar-ing my   life. __

_____   Ooh _____   Yeah

Ooh _____   Oh _____   yeah

FIG. II.20. Pop-R&B Melody

EXERCISE 21. BELTING LONG HIGH NOTES

This exercise, improvised by Erica Leonard in Video Example 21, shows how using an open vowel makes belting much smoother. Again, when you work with the sing-along track, feel free to try out different vowels, text, and runs. Experiment with different keys, higher and lower.

55–57   21

FIG. II.21. Belting Long High Notes

EXERCISE 22. MINOR PENTATONIC RIFFING

A simple, basic rock or R&B groove that has lots of room for you to work with. Watch Video Example 22 to see Jenna Glatt start with this phrase, then develop her phrasing in the moment to build a really exciting vocal. This sing-along track is easily looped to give you a long accompaniment to work with. Be sure you experiment with lower keys, too.

58 – 60   22

FIG. II.22. Minor Pentatonic Riffing

EXERCISE 23. MINOR KEY RIFFING 1, HIGH AND BRIGHT

This exercise provides a loop in the online sing-along that is very flexible. Start with the melody provided sung twice, then get creative. Try beginning low in your range, then building your riffs to travel higher into your belt. If you don't like what you sang the first go-round, try something else!

61 – 63   23

FIG. II.23. Minor Key Riffing 1

EXERCISE 24. MINOR KEY RIFFING 2

This is the riff example sung by David Keck in Video Example 24, which he then varies up a little bit. Feel free to play around with the blues feel and changes to suit your taste, like adding salt and pepper to a recipe. Be sure you experiment with lower keys, too.

64 – 65   24

FIG. II.24. Minor Key Riffing 2

CONCLUSION

Throughout this book you have learned how to belt without harming your voice, been shown exercises to practice, and learned how your voice moves and shifts whenever you sing. Myths about belting have been debunked, replaced with facts and real-life practical applications. Hopefully this book has inspired you to approach belting with respect for your voice, and with high regard for the mental and physical stamina it takes to belt well.

The most important thing you must do to become really good at belting is practice. In the end, belting is a physical experience that you have to find within your own body. Remember to be patient, especially if this style of singing is new to you. Take time with the exercises. Watch the videos online and work with the online audio accompaniments. Always, *always* warm up your voice (and your body) adequately before you begin to belt. And, if you can, find a really good teacher to work with who understands the factual mechanics of the singing voice, and who gets you.

Most of all, have fun! Singing is a gift. When you share your singing voice with others, they have received a special part of what makes you *You*. If you ever get stressed out about how you sound, remember that there is always another opportunity to practice, to try again, to work on your craft.

ABOUT THE AUTHOR

Photo by Mark Stallings

Jeannie Gagné (gon-YAY) is a veteran professional vocalist, and long-time professor in the voice department at Berklee College of Music. With a graduate degree in advanced vocal technique and wellness (Lesley University, Cambridge), combined with decades of experience as a professional singer and skills as a Reiki master, Jeannie's specialty as a teacher is showing students how to gain power, style, and expression in numerous genres—while maintaining a healthy, vital instrument.

At Berklee, Jeannie designed and teaches vocal technique classes and workshops, as well as a unique science course that blends wellness studies with scientific fact to demonstrate how the body processes sound and music. She also teaches private voice lessons, performance classes, and bandleading in jazz, blues, pop/rock, country, singer/songwriter, R&B, and classical styles. A pianist and acoustic guitar player, Jeannie cofounded Berklee's Performance Wellness Institute for students and teachers of all instruments. Known widely for her YouTube series *The Vocal Genie*, she is sought out by singers worldwide for her expertise, humor, and caring teaching style.

Jeannie's solo albums *Closer to Bliss, Must Be Love*, and *Wide Open Heart* feature some of the industry's most respected musicians. Her songwriting reflects life's journey, the ups and the downs, ultimately concluding that we are blessed to be here. Throughout her career she has been fortunate to work with truly phenomenal musicians including Philip Glass and Ravi Shankar, George Duke, Barenaked Ladies, for NBC-TV with comedians Penn and Teller, Livingston Taylor, Walter Beasley, Terri Lyne Carrington, Shawn Pelton (SNL, Sheryl Crow), Everett Bradley (Springsteen, Swing! on Broadway), Zev Katz (Sting, Aretha Franklin), reggae legend Frankie Paul and many more. She is featured on the soundtracks for feature films including *Anima Mundi, Forbidden Nights*, and *Feuille*, on NPR's *All Things Considered*, the *CBS Evening News, People* magazine, by New York City TV, and by numerous news outlets.

Jeannie is also the author of *Your Singing Voice: Contemporary Technique, Expression and Spirit* (2012), which stresses a mind-body approach to contemporary singing, wellness, and personal authenticity. For more information about Jeannie Gagné and her music, visit: www.jeanniegagne.com and www.thevocalgenie.com.